Gisela Daum

Die besten englischen Filserbriefe
Your true Gisela

Gisela Daum

Die besten englischen Filserbriefe

Your true Gisela

Herausgegeben von
Egbert von Meckinghoven

Mit Illustrationen von
Felix Weinold

Langen Müller

Besuchen Sie uns im Internet unter
http://www.langen-mueller-verlag.de

1. Auflage März 2000
2. Auflage November 2001 – Sonderproduktion
3. Auflage September 2002 – Sonderproduktion
4. Auflage Februar 2003 – Sonderproduktion
5. Auflage März 2003 – Sonderproduktion

© 2000 by Langen Müller in der
F. A. Herbig Verlagsbuchhandlung GmbH, München
Alle Rechte vorbehalten
Schutzumschlag: Wolfgang Heinzel
Umschlagzeichnung: Felix Weinold, Schwabmünchen
Herstellung und Satz: VerlagsService Dr. Helmut Neuberger
& Karl Schaumann GmbH, Heimstetten
Gesetzt aus der 10,5/13 Punkt New Caledonia
Druck und Binden: GGP Media, Pößneck
Printed in Germany
ISBN 3-7844-2777-4

Inhalt

Zum Geleit 7

Vorwort des Herausgebers 9

Moderne Zeiten 11

Freud und Leid im Alltag 41

Britischer geht's nicht 61

Deutsches Wesen und die Welt 87

Gesund und schön 115

Ökologie für den Hausgebrauch 137

Liebe, Lust und Frust 157

Aus der Traumfabrik 175

Es weihnachtet sehr 189

Politisches, allzu Politisches 205

Ausführliches Inhaltsverzeichnis 234

Zum Geleit

„Das Englische ist eine einfache,
aber schwere Sprache. Es besteht
aus lauter Fremdwörtern, die
falsch ausgesprochen werden."
Kurt Tucholsky

„Der unter deutschen Gebildeten
am meisten verbreitete Aberglaube
ist der, daß sie Englisch könnten."
Johannes Gross

"Believe me, it is so!"
Arthur Schopenhauer

"I think this is quite a self-understanding
fact that I am here. Why should I not do it
as landchief of a neighbouring state?"
Franz Josef Strauß
vor der internationalen Presse
anläßlich eines überraschenden
Besuchs in Leipzig zu DDR-Zeiten

Vorwort des Herausgebers

Are you heavy on wire, or are you on the woodway?
Equal goes it loose – fast jeder in Deutschland kennt
solche und ähnlich grotesken Direktübersetzungen,
die den Englischlehrer zur Weißglut oder auf die
Palme bringen können: *They bring him to white-glow
or on the palm tree.* Allerdings gibt es an manchen
Schulen auch schon fortschrittlichere Pädagogen, die
an der haarsträubend komischen Sprachspielerei ge-
nauso Gefallen finden wie ihre Schülerinnen und
Schüler. Gemeinsam arbeiten sie heraus, daß Englisch und Deutsch zwei verschiedene Sprachsysteme
mit unterschiedlichen Sprachbildern und Redewen-
dungen sind.

Um so mehr fordern die Ähnlichkeiten, die beide
Sprachen miteinander verbinden, neben Jux und Dol-
lerei zu erhöhter Wachsamkeit und Sensibilität heraus. Doch diese Warnung wird von deutscher Seite
viel zu häufig in den Wind geschrieben. Englisch?
Englisch kann doch jeder! Im Ernstfall fragt man sich
in London auf folgende Weise durch: *Excusen's me,
where goes it here long to the Piccadilly Circus?* Dies
wurde nicht frei erfunden, sondern im O-Ton er-
lauscht.

In einem Englisch, das eigentlich kein Englisch ist
und das die Deutschen besser verstehen können als
die Engländer, schreibt nun eine gewisse Gisela ihrem in London ansässigen Freund Peter in unermüd-
licher Emsigkeit. Wie alles anfing? Der erste Brief

VORWORT DES HERAUSGEBERS

von *Your true Gisela* erschien am 17. März 1984 auf der „Letzten Seite" der Wochenendausgabe der *Süddeutschen Zeitung*, und zwar als „Englischer Filserbrief". Diese Überschrift, die zum unverkennbaren Markenzeichen der alle vier bis sechs Wochen erscheinenden Kolumne geworden ist, spielt auf eine bekannte literarische Figur des Volksschriftstellers Ludwig Thoma an, nämlich auf Jozef Filser. Der königlich-bayerische Landtagsabgeordnete aus der Provinz setzt sich nach getaner Arbeit hin, verfaßt Briefe und schickt sie nach Hause – frisch von der Leber weg und frei, wie ihm der Schnabel gewachsen ist. Sie handeln von seinem schwierigen und aufreibenden Beruf, der ihn oft überfordert, von persönlichen Problemen und skurrilen Abenteuern in der Großstadt München.

Was die trockene Art, den gelegentlich derben Humor und die satirischen Seitenhiebe auf den Zeitgeist betrifft, so besteht sicherlich eine innere Verwandtschaft zwischen Jozef Filser und *Your true Gisela*. Kein Thema und kein Kalauer wird ausgelassen; es geht um Kitsch und Kultur, um Adel und Politik, um Gott und die Welt. Mit ihrem völlig unbekümmerten Filser-Englisch fängt *Your true Gisela* gerade auch solche Momente des Alltagslebens ein, in denen wir uns freud- und leidvoll wiedererkennen können.

Im Dezember 1999

Egbert von Meckinghoven

Moderne Zeiten

What is lifestyle?

FAST EINE LEBENSBERATUNG

Dear Peter,

all world takes the word lifestyle into the mouth, even in our German speech. But what means it now real? Is it to byplay a sign of lifestyle, when a man himself always with a three-days-beard under's folk begives and he himself sowith not from an ordinary beggar or land-striker off-lifts? Can be, can not be; knows the vulture. So have I me about-looked and this and that to the clearing of the question together-collected, what all under lifestyle to understand is. Some real lifestyle-experts like my friend Gerda or Cousin Walter made my underseekings easier. I have them both very to thank.

What kind of parties you give, is a safe sign of your lifestyle. It makes a great, not to say an enormous difference, if you an authentic champagne original out Reims in France come let or only a cheap belch-water out German lands, called *Sekt*, on the table of the house put. Authentic is a whole, whole important beat-word in this togetherhang, every shit must anyhow authentic be. Besorrow you to byplay an LP (no, *not* a CD) with authentic Georgian songs – no, not from America, but out Georgia southly of the Kaukasus. And bring Georgia as a constant factor in every deep-exploring political discussion in. Your guests bewonder your intelligence and your fine-feeling – also when they nothing of Georgia understand and fore

– 13 –

MODERNE ZEITEN

the music on lovest away run would. But this do they
not, they remain teeth-grinding. Georgian songs are
namely not after everyman's taste. Become please no
horror, but all this is an expression of lifestyle. The
outfallener, the better.

Quite important: The eat-portions must very, very
small be. A tiny piece of salmon with a half mince-leaf
is enough. Large portions would show, that you quite
cheap inbought have. Crocodile-eggs, to byplay, are in
dozen cheaper – too cheap for a lifestyle-aspirant. As
we by the eating are: Beat yourself never simple your
stomach full, also then not, when it you tastes and you
thereafter is. This would no sign of lifestyle be. The
talking *over* the eating is mindest evenso important
like the eating self. When you in this tosight on the
running be will, is it un-he-letly, that you bestandy the
column of Wolfram Siebeck read, this after like before
unhereached time-taster. He says you on highest in-
tellectual level (as we newerthings in German say),
but very clip and clear, where the time-ghost long
goes and when the lifestyle a quite other direction
takes.

A warning: Read not *Life & Style*, *InStyle* or *Joy* –
that is away-thrown money. These sonamed lifestyle-
magazines run only all trends after. Today this, to-
morow that. These gazettes are highest prothetics for
those poor drops and infold's brushes, who not self instand are, out their innerest inner self a real lifestyle
to *live*. And that is quite, quite sad.

Lifestyle is, when you *not* by Aldi shopping go,
ifwell some lifestyle-freaks middlerwhile of other
meaning are. A little caviar for the broad folk makes

– 14 –

FAST EINE LEBENSBERATUNG

still no lyfestyle out. What real counts: By Aldi have they only one sort of whisky. Now could you freely say, you need only one sort. But lifestyle is, when you your sort from 56 sorts of whisky outseek can – now comes it – self, when it exact the sort out the Aldi be should. This is not only lifestyle, but abovetherein *personal* lifestyle.

Lifestyle is overhead all, what you buy can – to by-play the song from the Beatles "Money can't buy me love". But what always you also buy, I ask you: Have a sorrow-foldy look thereon, that it not just *Hinz* and *Kunz* also buy can. What you *not* buy can, is general no lifestyle: a handknit pullover or shawl from your friend, a selfmade calendar, a handwritten love-letter or an unawaited beautifull sun-undergang. When you but to Bali travel and a guarenteed wonderfull sun-undergang for every day booked have, then is that again lifestyle. Have you it checked?

Your true Gisela

– 15 –

Beer on wine

EIN GUTES TRÖPFCHEN

Dear Peter,
have I you written, what for an outspoken wine-love-
haver my Cousin Walter is? He knows all wines in the
world. In his cellar governs an order, which you only
picobello name can. First the wine-regions, then
come the single yeargangs. Every day controls he the
temperature in the cellar. Thereby is it for his red
wines much too cold there, says he. What for a luck,
that he not so much red wine drinks, but overweigh-
ing white wine, special the German *rieslings*.

Last week were my friend Gerda and I by Walter inloaded. Thereby were we not only new-greedy on his
new wine-depot, but this time also on his new flame,
who on the beautifull name Miriam hears. To make it
short, before I wider into the details go: Miriam was
and is total o.k., but the wine-probe with the afterplay
was like a piece out the horror-cabinet.

Without our nice flowers out to pack, which we him
extra as a little present with-brought had, began Walter with the be-teaching: To all-first comes it on the
flower of the wine on. He opened a bottle, held it
under the nose, sniffed like a dog, closed his eyes,
smiled and came into swarming. Us ladies ran the
water in the mouth together, but this expert filled only
his glass and slurfed the wine alone. Abrupt said he:
No ... is it then the possibility? Yes, it was openbar the
possibility: Loud Walter had this wine more flower

– 16 –

EIN GUTES TRÖPFCHEN

than bouquet. That means, he smelled fuller than he tasted. What for a catastrophe!

In the between-time would I me a cigarette onstick, when Walter very protested: No, that goes not on a wine-probe, also no strong perfume (godbethank had I not to my Chanel 19 gripped or to a heavier weapon) and nothing sharp, better overhead nothing to eat. That could yes serene become! No salt-poles, no earth-nuts, no cheese, no student's food – Walter set us only bone-dry white-bread before the nose. And how this tastes, must I you not tell. That would yes mean: White-bread to England carry.

With the second wine had we more luck, Walter made us the glasses quarter-full. A good drop, would I say, could man also allday's drink – a little bit furry in the after-taste freely. But Walter bestood thereon, that he fruity and full was, bynear fiery and racy. Yes, when Walter that says. We found not the right words, and Walter made us clear: You must him under the tongue become – anyhow came me this beknown fore.

By the third wine offered Miriam us the you on, and we drank brotherhood – or was it *sisterhood* in this fall? Then shattered we the nice song: Why is it on the Rhine so beautifull? Yes why? Gerda gave to understand, that her this wine like the second tasted. Wrong, said Walter (this clever-shitter), like the first! But there could we not more withhold. The more we drank, the lustier became the evening. With the fourth wine, which not my thing was, watered I Walter's flower-pots. But naturely not before his eyes.

The fifth wine was unhomely grassy and the sixth a bit aromatic and still very, very piquant. The flower

– 17 –

MODERNE ZEITEN

was in order, and we had a flag, which itself washed had. But that played overhead no violin more – the thirst would and would not way-go. And I can you this tell: Thirst is worse than home-woe.

Tohome took I two bottles beer to me, a cold cutlet and a tomato, but I had a sleeploose night. What wonder, how says namely the folk's mouth? Beer on wine, that let be! I felt me like on a carousel. The next time drink I first two litres beer against the thirst. Then gives it so good like no problems: Wine on beer, that rate I you!

This is an old German folk's wisdom. Know you this also in England?

Your true Gisela

A picture for the gods

PIZZA: TAG UND NACHT

Dear Peter,
it gives days, there are you total groggy, when you evening's from the work homecome. Fix and foxy. The colleagues went you the whole day on the cakes, underway's came a sin-flood of rain down, the stocking had a running mesh, and the police told you, that you fourteen comma seven kilometres too quick was. In such moments know I only one: feet high, TV onswitch and the channels up and down zap.

But after a while announces himself an animalish hunger to word. No wonder, by all this reclame for cheese and chocolate, noodles and soups, beer and cola, ice-cream and pudding. Eye in eye with such a fata morgana, runs you formly the water in the mouth together. A look into the cool-cupboard makes me freely quite quick clear, that I nothing from these wonderfull things inbought have. What find I? Only one and a half tomato, an off-run strawberry-yoghurt, total sour milk and a piece butter from anno tobac.

What do? To cook had I also no lust. There fell me in, that my friend Gerda shortly from a new Italian restaurant swarmed has. She was so very beghosted from this Giovanni and his cook-art, that he – me nothing, you nothing to her stem-local upclimbed is. But should I me now on the socks make? In this rain – I, mother-soul's alone? No, on no fall, not for money

MODERNE ZEITEN

and good words. By such a weather send you no dog before the door.

But there know you the Giovanni bad. Clever is he, unhomely clever. He has not only a good-going restaurant, but for the need-falls also a pizza-taxi. So gripped I to the telephone, and soforth was the chief on the apparatus. It came to the following dialogue: Hello Giovanni, can you me well a pizza bring, before I fore hunger dead am? *Si, si, Gisela, what may it be?* Hm, I thought the number eleven – with much paprika and cheese thereon, but without this horrible knofel. *Null problemo, Gisela, subito, ciao.*

In wind's hurry stood Giovanni with the pizza before my door in the fourth stock. The smell was much promising. And real: no knofel, which me on the palm bring would. But what must my inflamed eyes see, when I the warm carton opened? I say you, a middler catastrophe! And this came so: You must halt know, that the Giovanni not just a car drives, but a super-hot oven his own calls. A Ferrari or a Lamborghini, when you this what says. Seldom takes he the foot from the gas-pedal, and in-follow-of-that goes he with rasant tempo into the curves. And when it be must, treads he full on the brakes, there knows he nothing. He understands this a test for his brakes, says he, which man not often enough make can.

Now is the Giovanni with the seat-belt fast on his seat fastened, but the pizza yes not – special not the paprika and the mushrooms, also not the tomatoes and the cheese on the pizza. In clear-text: The belay was absolute not more on the pizza to find, but accurate over the whole inner carton distributed. It was

– 20 –

PIZZA: TAG UND NACHT

hard work for me, the eating out the carton to stem. You had me poor girl see should – a picture for the gods.

Man oh man, the next time throw I the oven on and make me self an orderly pizza!

Your true Gisela

The undergang of the evening-land

DIE NEUE KULTUR DES ESSENS

Dear Peter,
from the hand in the mouth, the nose over the papp-plate: eating in standing, under free heaven and the ellbows of other people bestandy in the back. That is it, that is total chic, also when the mayo or the ketcup over your jacket drops. Who with the time goes, eats with the fingers and whistles what on knife and fork.

And this happens not homely – to byplay when I in the night still quick in the cool-cupboard grip (before I in the night on hunger die). No, in all public come the fingers to honour, equal what served is: sausage or pizza, hamburger or rollmops, schaschlik or chicken, döner or doughnut, pancake or pommes. Practisher goes it yes now real not. The fingers, which man at the end of the procedure off-lick can, has man yes always and overall thereby!

And all people make with, without onseen of the person: workers and professors, yuppies and skin-heads, farmers and ministers, girls and boys. I say you what: The most children today know not more, what a bestick is. Some museums have collections and offer courses under the title: How hold I a bestick correct in hands? But this is only what for unbeteachable tra-ditionalists or for people, who in the history of bygone times interested are.

Today blows an other wind. Some people set them-selves for the eating on a bank, when they one find. If

– 22 –

DIE NEUE KULTUR DES ESSENS

not, then is it a *Stehimbiß*. But the footganger-zones in our towns and cities are full of eaters, who not only in standing a pizza or a portion of gyros between the teeth push, but also while they are walking. Some people come thereby with only one hand out, in the other hand carry they namely a shopping-bag or a handy. For this art-piece need you only a fast grip.

No body eats more to home. And while this so is, find we landup, landdown hundreds of markets, which the most people only for the *Fraß* beseek (is it *grub* in English?): week- and year-markets, christ-childerl- and flea-markets. Every three metres an other stand. Alone the smell of different sorts of burnt fat is a fantastic adventure for the nose. Or a torture.

All this shows: The undergang of the evening-land is near. But were we not so proud, that we not more on the trees sit? Shall all civilization forgotten be? I have still learned, that man only to seldom occasions with the fingers eat can – to byplay by the camping, angling, paddling or wandering. In the open landscape can you yourself your butter-bread out the fist taste let, without that you someone a rope thereout turns.

I must freely togive, that some time-companions it into the other direction overdrive and a seldsome idea of a picnic have. They can not others, than a snow-white table-cloth on the grass out to broad and knife and fork with to bring. And also under free heaven bestand they on two sorts of glasses, one for the red wine, the other for the white wine. Form-fullended.

What for problems! The cannibal of today beseeks all the while these sonamed restaurants, where you

– 23 –

MODERNE ZEITEN

absolute no other chance have than with your fingers to eat. A bestick is fullcome unbeknown. Children bego there feastly their birthday: Happy Hamburger to you! When will we there a Mc-Wedding-Eating off-hold?

And when will Wolfram Siebeck there a test make?

Your true Gisela

The purest terror

WENN DAS TELEFON KLINGELT

Dear Peter,
everytime, when I so there sit and nothing bad think, when I me the "Dream Wedding" with Linda de Mol onlook, when I a good book read, when I so quite relaxed my fir-needle-bath take, when I my yoga-exercises after me bring or when I simple my rest have will – then passeers it guaranteed: Loudstark makes itself the telephone bemarkbar.

My first thought: Shit what thereuopon, I am not there. All my friends know, when I to speak am and when not. Who can it be? But some time-companions are yes so hardnecky, that you the holy anger become can. They let the telephone jingle and jingle, so that a real mightfight begins. Who has the stronger nerves?

Last end's become you with-sorrow. Muchlight is a friend in trouble and needs your help. And could it not be, that you the head-winner in a price-out-writing are and already a flight-trip to Barbados in the pocket have? That can man not on the long bank push, that needs initiative. I take the hearer up and say: "Yes?" (Thereby hate I, when people on the telephone "yes" say and not their name.) And who is it in the most falls? Someone, who you in the soul not outstand can, or some poor drop: "Sorry, I have the false number elected."

It is the purest terror! My friend Gerda makes the whole circus not more with. "Must I always for Hinz

– 25 –

MODERNE ZEITEN

and Kunz parat stand, live I then only for the telephone?" gave she newly from her. The end from the song: She has newerthings an automatic call-beanswerer. But is this now the Egg of the Columbus? I say you: By wide not! For the caller may such a machine only optimal be. Man sits letty there and lets the whole world on band speak – when this everybody withmakes. By me to byplay go soforth the jalousies down, when I a call-beanswerer on the ear have. I am so unhomely nervous and begin to stotter, when I hear: "Speak now!" or "Speak after last peep-tone!" I bring no sentence tostand and hang lover the hearer in. Shall the other himself who knows what think. Headthing, he or she makes himself not lusty over me.

But one great forepart has the telephone, all what right is: Man can the blue from heaven lie, and the other sees not, how man red in the face becomes. And what some people so on the telephone tell, would they in life not from face to face say. Aunt Lissy to byplay asks me only on the telephone, why I always still as single live and when I on the thought came, a man the yes-word to give. Witty, what?

But when you me ask, am I so or so more for's letter-writing. So shall we two it also wider hold, not true?

Your true Gisela

– 26 –

You, I am now here

SEGEN UND FLUCH DES HANDY

Dear Peter,

have you also bemarked, that a new type of time-companion under us is? Middlerwhile are these modern men and women unoverseebar, who in all publicity such a cucumber on the ear press. The show-finger of the other hand holds the other ear fast to. The look goes fullcome into the emptiness. What I mean? Where these people go and stand, have they permanent a mobile telephone thereby – in the railway and in the bus, in the restaurant and on the street, in the theatre and and in the concert, in the church and in the cinema, on the wedding and on the be-earthning, in forest and on the heath. Nowhere on the whole wide world can you these days before these handy-people safe be. It cries to heaven.

By every business is the handy thereby, in bed and bath, even on the WC. Newly, when I such a pressure on the blow had, that I it not longer outhold could, fell me a stone from the heart, that a WC in sight was. But beset, shit. You believe it not. For-true sat there a lady on the pot and talked over her handy in all soul-rest about this and that with her friend. And I stood there and stepped from one leg on the other. Why can these handy-people not into a normal telephone-cell go or thereto, where the pepper grows?

It is a land-plague. What not all must I unfreewilly with-hear, what he or she brew-warm and loudstark

– 27 –

MODERNE ZEITEN

into the handy speaks. Whole mankind-dramas and personal relation-kists, who earlier absolute private were, are now shame-loose before our all ears out-broaded – if you will or not. I become rule-massy a crisis, when me a person with handy under the eyes comes. But these handy-users have nerves like steel-cables. They are total hardnecky – horribler than a smoker in a non-smoker-zone.

Greatest part's is the communication freely so sow-stupid, that I me on the head grip and ask: Why about everything in the world must this information exact in this eye-look over the ether go? Who is it on the other end, who nothing betters to do has, than to byplay messages like these in reception to take: "Where are you? ... You, I am now here ... Yes, I hear you also good ... Yes, no, yes ... Till later, treasure ... All clear, ciao." As if we it only with sparrow-brains to do had.

When my friend Gerda shopping goes, is she always with plastic-bags underways – groundsetly. After a while knows she naturely not, in which of her thousand bags now the handy sticks. In the rule plays this no violin. But woe, when the handy peeps. Then goes the seeking loose. I say you, this must you see. It peeps and peeps, and the peeping takes first then an end, short *before* the silly thing found is. What for a desaster.

And know you, why my Cousin Walter a handy be-sits? Newly said he to me: "When I with my Landrover in Sotland on a lonely field-way stand and my friend in Rome in a fashion-show sits, can I her call and her the sun-undergang in all details be-write." Yes really, that is it.   *Your true Gisela*

– 28 –

SEGEN UND FLUCH DES HANDY

P.S. Newly saw I a man before a bank, who his handy used, while he with his other hand the money out the money-automat pulled. Quite clear, time is money. For busy people like him have I my newest invention parat – a handy with an in-built dry-shaver.

Place there, now come I!

GELÄNDEWAGEN ODER BESSER: OFF-ROAD

Dear Peter,
to this year's time, when the sun higher stands, come by good weather bynear all people out their holes – great and little, poor and rich, thick and thin. With fore-love makes man an outflight to Mother Nature. What can nicer, healthier and greener be? Many people go tofoot, some climb on the bike. But the broad mass is with the car underway's. What Mother Nature thereto says, is them shit-equal. Headsake, these nature-love-havers goes it good.

And then gives it there a species of car-besitters, who with their drivable under-sentence not near enough to the bosom of Mother Nature come can. Already with a fully normal car can you the normal forest-ways up and down thunder. The question is only, if these people normal are. Who this not crazy enough finds, buys himself a special car – my Aunt Lissy would say a "jeep". But with this outprint out the war's time can you by these people today not land. The correct besigning of it is "off-road" – how we newerthings in German say.

It is clear like thick ink: For crossing rivers and climbing mountains is naturely a special car good to use. So an off-road-bolide has namely a direct drive on all four wheels. And a colossal bumper on the front, with which you a herd of fight-lusty nose-horns flat make can. When I freely honest am: Together with

– 30 –

GELÄNDEWAGEN ODER BESSER: OFF-ROAD

their chrome-parts look these unhandly cars out like American overland-trucks, which by the cook-wash-gang inshrinked are.

Joke byside. The springing point is halt, that these hot ovens seldom for a safari over fields and meadows used are, but quasi out-closely for boulevard-cruising on our city-roads: Shopping on the market, seeking a park-place near the fitness-studio or just up and down the road. Only once so, just to make impression. I say you: This trend is absolute "in" – from Munich to Hamburg, from Gütersloh to Görlitz. Middlerwhile count we by us say and write one million of these "cruisers", "patrollers", "discoverers" and "troopers".

There can man yes only happy be, that Mother Nature under such pure ongivers not so much to suffer has. But what will us this car-type then really say? What about all in the world? Is such a clapper-box in our cities not so overflowing like a fold-boat in the Sahara? Think you. The simple message, when such a monster of a vehicle into your look-field comes, is clip and clear: Place there, now come I!

And then, when you your life love is, make you place for the rambo. Or you hold your car nice on, even if you green on the ample have. With open mouth and fullcome freewilly naturely ...

Your true Gisela

– 31 –

Nothing like away from here

AUF ZUM BALLERMANN!

Dear Peter,
the summers in this our land have their name real not earned. Naturely comes the one or the other hot day in our broads fore, but mostest falls the weather so out, how it our great poet and thinker Heinrich Heine with pregnant words bewritten has: "The summers in Germany are only green-painted winters." No wonder, that our land's people in masses into the south stream, where the inhomish people eye-shinely a better wire than we to St. Petrus have.

Freely am I in the rule not for long travels who knows whereto to have. All in all find I my fatherland very beautifull, special here in Bavaria. But when it newly once again out all buckets shedded, overfell me a panic. Wet to the bones after a horrible shower, thought I only of my before-standing holidays and became prompt a crisis. Only one idea went me steady through the head – summer, sun and beach. Nothing like away from here!

Flight's begave I me into a travel-bureau, where me to ears came, that I a bit late thereon was. *Last Minute* was the device – as we newerthings wordwordly in German say. In ghost saw I me already on Gran Canaria, in the Dominican Republic, in Sri Lanka or on Mauritius. It was me equal, headsake summer, sun and beach. In last minute landed I on Mallorca.

AUF ZUM BALLERMANN!

I will it not under the carpet sweep: Tofirst had I many bethinkings – cleanwoman-island, *Ballermann* and so. But what for Boris Becker and Claudia Schiffer, Peter Maffay and Sabine Christiansen, Michael Douglas and Frédéric Chopin good enough is, should for me only right and cheap be. These prominents and number-rich would-like-to-be-prominents have halt on Mallorca their tents for always up-beaten – Frédéric Chopin to byplay in the beautifull mountain-village Valldemossa. What shall I say – temperatures, water and beach were full in order. "Full" is overhead the right word. It came me so fore, as if this year all world on Mallorca holiday makes. Who counts the peoples, knows the names, who guestly here together-came? I see this total positive: Innerhalf of minutes learn you dozens of fully different persons know.

But the best of Mallorca is, that you yourself complete like to home feel can. The pubs carry names like "Münchner Kindl", "Schluckspecht", "Futterkrippe" or "Mozart II". The main steets are the "Bierstraße" and the "Schinkenstraße". In the restaurants stand *Eisbein* with *Sauerkraut*, *Grillhaxen*, *Currywurst* and *Jägerschnitzel* on the card. The serving speaks a halfway's understandable German. You must nothing miss – not the good German beer out Munich or Warstein and not the excellent German filter-coffee with this unbewritable *Verwöhnaroma*. Heart, what will you more? A bit hinderly, when not paradox is it othersides, that you always with *Pesetas* pay and in *Pesetas* think must. Were it not easier and only consequent, when Mallorca one day's our seventeenth federal land be would?

– 33 –

MODERNE ZEITEN

The mega-event is but a night-beseek in the beer-cellar "Oberbayern". Already the whole day see you Spaniards dressed in leather-trousers, white-blue t-shirts and with blue hair, who for this local reclame make. Up goes it with music from finest: Costa Cordalis, Wolgang Petry and Roland Kaiser. And then is Polonaise Blankenese onsaid – in goose-march goes it over stools, tables and banks. But the absolute high-point is the election of "Miss Oberbayern". There-against comes me the "Hofbräuhaus" in Munich like a cloister fore.

After fourteen days were my most costbar weeks of the year foreby. Shall I you honest say, what I on the last day to me said? Nothing like away from here!

Your true Gisela

P.S. Two Germans meet a Mallorquinese man near the *Ballermann 6* on Mallorca. The man understands the two not. Says the one German to the other: "You, he is not from here."

You can say you to me

ENGLISCH? NICHTS LEICHTER ALS DAS!

Dear Peter,
is it real, real true – you me here in Munich beseek
come will? I can it still not begrip, I am total flat! Now
gives it naturely many things, over which you and I together afterthink must. So light is that yes not. My
Aunt Lissy says always: Other peoples, other cultures.
And as you self to expression bring, will you in every
situation unbethinged a good impression behind you
let. That find I very tactfull and toforecoming of you.
Before all shows itself special by table, who a good
child-room had and who not. But fine manners can
from folk to folk total different be, knows the cuckoo.
The first ground-rule is: Look in the round, what the
others so do. Then make also you nothing wrong. Take
the fork in the left hand, and the knife in the right. In
England is yes well all others. We to byplay drive on
the right side of the street. Not that I think, that you
Englanders on the wrong side of the street drive. But
be eightsome, when you here over the street go. The
vehicles come guaranteed from the side, into which
you not look. And in null comma nothing are you
under a car.

Back to the table. Before you one bite into the
mouth put, must you the others a good appetite wish
– even if you no appetite have or if the meal not so ap-
petitely outlooks. Thereon lay we heretoland great
worth. Others than in England, may you the potatoes

MODERNE ZEITEN

not with the knife cut. When you are spoonig the soup with the one hand, is it you not allowed, that the other hand under the table-cloth hangs. The people could yes God-knows-what from you think. Please make a nice fist with this hand and lay it elegant on the table.

When you what on the plate become, say you *Danke!* Otherfalls can it be, that you hear must: Yes, what says man then? And give always the hand, so that it orderly be shaken can. It should the right hand be, the nice hand. Be not shocked, we Germans mean it always only good with you. When you per tofall the left hand given have, is this no leg-break. Say then with a smile: The left comes from heart. This shows, that you wit and a good portion humour besit.

When you a person around midday meet, say you always *Mahlzeit!* Ask me not after the why. The other person answers you also with *Mahlzeit*, and there see you soforth, that you not on the woodway are. The oversetting of the word is "mealtime", but in reality means it nothing. Be foresighty with the begreeting here in Bavaria. When you in the rest of Germany under normal circumstances simply with *Guten Tag* toright-come, must you know, that the blue-white standard-greeting *Grüß Gott* is. With this "Greet God" document we daydayly from mornings to evenings before all world, that we a part of the christly-catholic evening-land are. And this can you not from every folk say, first rigth not from our brothers and sisters, who northly of the White-Sausage-Equator live.

When you as man with a lady the stairs high-go, let her on no fall as first go – outer she has jeans on.

– 36 –

ENGLISCH? NICHTS LEICHTER ALS DAS!

Otherfalls could you a look under her rock throw, and this is not correct and sendly. The problem is but, that you now into enormous conflict come with an other elementary rule. We Germans say namely wordwordly: *Ladies first!* This rule has absolute fore-rank – only not on the stairs. You can therein a certain fine-feeling see, of which you perhaps not thought had, that this the Germans to own is.

Also make we a great difference between you and you. There have you Englanders absolute no shimmer from. I mean, we say *Du* to a friend, a good beknown or familiar person, and we say *Sie* to every strange person. But the most people are here so friendly, that you as a stranger after three or four beers throughout hear can: I am the Schorsch, you can say you to me. It is so natural and so charming. In the northly Germany must you with a person first a sack salt eat, before it so wide comes.

Your true Gisela

They whistle you what!

NEUES BAUEN IN DER KRITIK

Dear Prince Charles,

your book "A Vision of Britain" is very interesting, but know you, what you there from the fence broken have? A war, namely a war against the most sensible human beings, which you on this earth find can: the architects. A prince or a mimosa is nothing there-against.

You can what against the Pope or the politicians say, against your Prime Minister or against our Federal President myways, but never against those people, who themselves as gods onsee. And do they what others, when they this world daily new create? Have the architects (each inch a fullprofi) it earned, that them an amateur the levites reads? What would you then say, when one of us on the idea came, loud thereover aftertothink, what a thrown-follower to do and to let has? Would *you* that right be?

I must togive: Here and there has the one or other architect not his best day had, when he on his pencil chewed and only the cigarbox new invented. But I think, with your critic go you much too wide. What louse is your majesty over the royal liver run, when you from modern buildings as "characterloose Frankenstein-monsters" speak? What can the poor Frankenstein therefore? You say, that more than 99% of the people behind you stand, when you in this form the architects the march blow. There falls me my

– 38 –

NEUES BAUEN IN DER KRITIK

greatmother in, who always said: People, eat more shit, millions of flies can not err and on the wrong way be!

When I you right understood have, lay you great worth thereon, that the architects "our climatic conditions" respect. Yes, you have so right: Through many a flat-roof dribbles also today still the rain through, that it to heaven cries. This must not be, but shall every modern building thathalf unbethinged a saddle-roof have? The World Trade Center in New York or Lloyd's in London with a saddle-roof? That I not laugh ... Then would it yes better outsee, when the Westminster Abbey a flat-roof had.

And then want you villages overall, with nice little houses and gardens rings around, also in the towns. The whole world one village, what a wonderful vision! But there should you to byplay the owners of a little piece of land middle in the city of London ask, what they from this idea hold. I am safe: They whistle you what!

And openbar has your majesty it not needy, great over any form of rendite aftertothink. Price-question: Who brings then the architects thereto, in some places so high and so massive to build? When your majesty the right answer on this question finds, can we the war-axe bebury and together the peace-pipe smoke. What hold you therefrom?

Your true Gisela

– 39 –

Freud und Leid im Alltag

Out of the tailor

SECHS RICHTIGE IM LOTTO

Dear Peter,
had you known, that the Germans a folk of luck's players are? Alone in Lotto give we bynear two-hundred
millions mark out – week for week, summers like winters. Lotto is a holy cow of the nation. It has what with
crosses to do. And it is so holy, that it in TV before the
"Word to Sunday" comes. I ask me allthethings, if this
really in the sense of the Holy Father is.

Will you in experience bring, how Lotto goes?
Nothing easier than that. You fill out a Lotto-shine,
inthem you just six numbers out forty-nine oncross
children-easy. That bring even those people, who not
write can and who only three crosses make as their
under-script. Then wait you, till your numbers pulled
are. While the chances on six rights not so good are,
can you perhaps till the year 3000 wait or still longer.
But this handicap makes the most tippers nothign out.
It plays no violin. When you not the right nerve for so
what have, is solikeso hop and malt lost. In this fall let
you better total the fingers therefrom. But when you
win, are you a luck's mushroom and out of the tailor.
And winners gives it every week.

My good old Aunt Lissy, who a fanatic Lotto-player
is, says always after the pulling: "Again such easy numbers, we could be under the winners!" She bandages
namely with every number something very personal.
Take the number-row from last week to byplay: 3, 4,

– 43 –

FREUD UND LEID IM ALLTAG

10, 25, 28, 41. To Aunt Lissy's birthday's dates pass the numbers 3 and 4. Know you, wherefor the 10 stands? It is the number of sisters and brothers of her first man Ludwig, 25 was his name's day (in August), 28 is her mother's death-day, and 41 is the house-number in her street, where her dog always stops and the leg lifts.

Know you, what Gustav, her second man, always said, when he still under the living whiled? Postmortal clever-shitting! But I think me so: Is it not pity, that she never the right numbers in fore-out say can?

But middlerwhile take we it halt easy. Even if you no pig in Lotto have, do you a good work. The half of the money goes to the poor sport or to old people. Or the state takes the half and brings therewith his household in order. This happens with the Lotto-moneys in our white-blue republic. That name I clever.

What is the fifth essence? Never was it so light, tomorrow a millionaire to be and today already a welldoer of mankind.

Your true Gisela

Big Brother lets greet

REKLAME, REKLAME, REKLAME

Dear Peter,
always, when I a look in my letter-box throw, is it most full. What gives it well news, is a letter from you thereby, lets muchlight the finance-office what positives hear? I could yes so happy be – so much post! Who likes not to become many letters and postcards? But when I the letter-box open, is the joy quick foreby: All only rubbish to all householdings – we call it post-throw-sending. That means: On best, you throw it direct way.

Until fore short was I so stupid to open every shit. From the outer upmaking was it often so upraining: An important personal message for you! Bar-money soforth!!! Your luck is in this enevelope! Can you the risk ingo, this letter not to open? I am alone for you there! In three days are you a millionaire! Open this letter soforth, you are under the head-winners!!! In one week had I alone 217 out-call-signs (!) counted. I am perplex: The most of the rubbish is quite alone for me, only for me personly, for nobody else. There exist openbar thousands of computers in our republic, which nothing others write than: Dear Miss or Mrs. Gisela Daum. What feel I me belly-brushed!

And what they me all as present overlet will, when I only what from them buy: key-etuis and fullfeather-holders, wine in sixer-pack, pictures from Rembrandt and van Gogh, golden bottle-openers and silvern

– 45 –

FREUD UND LEID IM ALLTAG

shoe-spoons. Or what I children-easy win can: a trip to the Fidschis and three Porsches – what shall I with three Porsches? The riddles are mostly from this sort: *Jed.r is. sei.e. G.ück.s .chm.ed!*

Now the hottest noodle: Shortly before Christmas had I what for the children-villages given – or was it Bread for the World (Cousin Walter adds always: But the sausage remains here). That had you seen should: As consequence came mindest three dozens of begging letters from all possible well-doing organizations. That have they them so thought! But not with me, man is yes no free-wild. There bedrive these post-throw-gangsters a blossoming commerce with my private address! Yes, where remains then there the date-protection?

Where am I overall now in the computers with these stitch-words: gives money for the poor, drinks expensive red-wine, reads critical magazines, likes some nerve-tickle (price-out-writing!) and chooses the Greens or highest the Sozis!

Big Brother lets greet ...

Your true Gisela

P.S. I besorrowed me extra a great, unoverseebar sticker for my letter-box: *Reclame inthrow forbidden!* But helped has it nothing. Can me perhaps somebody – please – from all this rubbish befree?

– 46 –

The last bite the dogs

HUNDE, WOLLT IHR EWIG LEBEN?

Dear Peter,

I can it not describe: Not the dogs, but these dog-holders go me sometimes on the nerves. Special, when I with friend Gerda my jogging make, comes one dog after the other, runs us after and makes a horrible noise. And always the dog-holder therebetween, loud crying: He does you nothing, he does you real nothing! He will only play!

If that the dogs knows? We can us very happy praise, when the dogs us not in the leg bite. That has us in the deed newly a dog-holder said. Should well a wit be. Also with his second wit had we so our difficulties: Better from dog in the leg bitten than from the stork – ha, ha, ha.

And then all the dog-shit. Unbelievable. When you not uppass, are you full with the foot therein. You must halt know, my new jogging-shoes have such a wonderfull profile-sole. Will you this theme with the dog-holders discuss, do they so, as if you air were. Or they give you snippish back: We pay so much dog-tax, that it to heaven cries. They hewait quite simple from this laugherly little tax, that the town-administration the shit way-makes – on best here and soforth, but hallo. What are these for people, who them selves animal-friends call, but quite forget, a people-friend to be. The sharpest: That they without bethinking the playplaces for children as dog-toilette onsee.

– 47 –

FREUD UND LEID IM ALLTAG

All were yes so easy with a plastic-bag and a little shovel. But this again sets foreout, that the dog-holders over the dog-shit real afterthink. Sometimes comes it me freely so fore, as if the dogs much cleverer are than *Herrchen* or *Frauchen*. Alone, how they with the dog speak: Waldi, come, come here … come you well here … place … I say place, sit, sit down … yes, what are you for a brave fellow … brave, Waldi, brave … no, not that, Waldi, let that … o no, *Frauchen* is quite sad …

I say only: Sad, sad, such a dog's life. How is the man on the dog come? How can it a dog-holder outhold, minutes-long by the onlined dog to stand, who every ten metres the shit from an other dog begood-eights? Why have the people dogs? That is one of the riddles of manhood. No dog knows it.

Godbethank have the most dogs a good character, what man from the people not so unbethinged behead should. As said: Not the dogs, the dog-holders can me the last nerve rob. The last bite the dogs.

Your true Gisela

Total oldmodish

LOBLIED AUF DAS FAHRRAD

Dear Peter,
to drive in a car today, makes not more much joy. The streets are overfilled, and the most time stand you there with the car and hear the traffic-through-says in the radio. We name this traffic-infarct. When you luck have and with your drivable under-sentence there are, where you wanted, exists there no parkplace for you. And when you after many rounds about the town a parkplace found have, must you fastput, that you not the right money for the park-clock thereby have. Damned shit!

In such situation come you muchlight on the idea: Must this all so be as it is? Gives it not what better's in life? Where is the Egg of the Columbus? Where is the clap, with which man two flies equal-timely beat can? I mean: to come a little quicker and comfortabler foreon than per pedes, but not with all this trouble of the car-drive.

The idea is: Two wheels are halt enough. And when you them out your own craft move, do you more for your health than in the car to sit, where you over short or long guaranteed a heart-infarct become. The Egg of the Columbus is the bike! I must say: I like my bike over alls. Ifwell it an old holland-bike is, which I from Aunt Lissy became, when her knees the bike-driving not more with made.

A holland-bike is the typical bike for a woman or a

– 49 –

girl. It is outspoken beautifull – total in black, but with white wheels. Every gentleman-bike can you against a holland-bike away-throw. There falls me in: Why is on the traffic-shield for bike-ways always only a gentleman-bike to see? In the time-older of the equal rights for all could tomindest every second shield a woman-bike show. Overhead: I find it absolute laugherly, how the men always their leg in the air swing, when they their bike in gang set.

And then besmear the men always the trousers with the oil from the chain. What have I it good with my holland-bike, that my chain complete in closed chain-box is. Also my rock has no chance, in the behind-wheel to come. A holland-bike has namely a special protection for woman. The saddle is a dream! Special, when you like I an outloading hinterpart have, come you therewith better toright than with these modern sport-saddles.

With my bike can I overall and everytime drive. There is never a stillstand like in a car. My bike-handler says freely, that my holland-bike fullcome olded is and that today what much better's on the market is. But shall I me on a mountain-bike swing and the whole nature and all wanderers unsafe make? Shall all world my crafty legs in leggings see?

No, this lifestyle is not after my cap. In this fall love I it, total oldmodish to be. On my old holland-bike let I nothing come!

Your true Gisela

Ripe for the clap's mill?

TOMATEN HABEN EINE SEELE

Dear Peter,
my Aunt Lissy is now over ninety. Here and there is it with her not more so as it earlier was – clear. One day is it the cross, the other days are it the knees, which not withmake will. But all in all is she quite good thereupon, special mental, as the Becker Boris say would. Lastendly plays itself all solikeso in the head off.

Aunt Lissy makes her own household so right and bad, with much help self-understandly from me and also, but quite seldom, from my Cousin Walter. Aunt Lissy loves crossword-riddles. She knows all rivers and side-rivers, all mountains, countries and all head-towns in the world.

But on lovest goes she into her garden to her tomatoes. And how her tomatoes taste! Fantastic! There throw you the taste-loose watersacks out Holland away. These genetic programmed time-bombs can me stolen be like the BSE-cows from England.

I wonder me but, it is me a total riddle, how Aunt Lissy that makes with her tomatoes. Opensightly has she a green thumb. But is there muchlight also a trick by? Who knows?

One morning's in last summer, when I by her overnighted, became I great eyes. First heard I a noise in the house. It was about six clock, and I thought with fear and horror: This must an inbreaker

– 51 –

FREUD UND LEID IM ALLTAG

be! But it was only Aunt Lissy, who upstood was. Me fell a stone from the heart. Through the opened window could I this true-take: My aunt went to the tomatoes and spoke to them with these words: How goes it you today? Have you good slept? Thereby touched she the plants quite soft with her hand. True-shinely says she also good-night to the tomatoes or sings an evening-song extra only for them.

Is Aunt Lissy mad, ripe for the clap's mill? Or have plants a soul, can they us feel? The beautifull ripe fruits give her right: Tomatoes need love. Or quite simple, the tomatoes follow the Beatles and will us say: *All you need is love!*

Had you so what from the tomatoes thought?

A whole while later read I in the newspaper, that also Prince Charles with his plants and trees speaks and that they before him down-bow, when he through his park lust-wandles. Next week will I it but know and it self outprobe. What Aunt Lissy and Prince Charles right is ...

Your true Gisela

All for the cat

ERLEBNIS AN DER TANKSTELLE

Dear Peter,

newly went me through the head, how it well so was, when it no carriable telephones, no computers and no credit-cards gave. What was that for a beautifull time, it must like in paradise have been! And today? I think, I live on an other star.

To byplay drove I youngest with my car to my tank-place. Must yes be from time to time, my old beatle is lastendly no perpetuum mobile. There fell me soforth into the eye: You can now your sprit with the EC-card be-pay. No cash, total easy, fullcome problem-loose. The tankward took my card, pressed me shorterhand a box in the hand and looked out the window. There should I my PIN ingive (the Personal Identity Number, as we newerthings in German say). And the rest goes from alone.

Think you! Was the PIN now 4117 or 4171 or 4711? Devil once more! The right numbers will not into my head – also not telephone-numbers, birthdays, post-sorrow-numbers. My friend Gerda noted her PIN direct on the card. How practish, why am I not so clever?

I probed it three times, the cold sweat broke me out. Endly had I luck. The cash-box spat the quittung out. I wrote only my day-kilometres up, how I that always so make.

To home wanted I outfind, how many litres my bea-

– 53 –

tle so per hundred kilometres swallows. That is me namely not equal. Man must yes always up-pass, therewith man self from the truest friend not over the ear beaten is. The overrushing could not greater be! I rubbed my eyes and looked and looked. The next adventure with the modern technique stood me before.

This was on the quittung to read: Naturely the date, the clock-time, the address of the tankward, his telephone, and the 55,42 DM for the sprit. But what had there a row of letters with numbers to seek, which for me Bohemian villages are – to byplay AID or AID-P or POS-Nr or TID? What says you 2302 or 703651? What shall the whole cheese? Thereby was the only information, which I real wanted, out-calculated *not* on the quittung to find: the litres which I tanked had. Total behammered! And I thought already, I musted my eye-doctor upseek.

The end from the song? Day for day is us told, that the forth-step not more up to hold is. But I ask you: Shall this really the forth-step be?

Is it not all for the cat?

Your true Gisela

When the cock crows on the mist

WEISHEIT DES WETTERBERICHTS

Dear Peter,

I bewonder you Englanders yes very, how you all problems of the allday on the light shoulder take. Think only of the weather. How hard are you there in taking! When it ice-cold is and me the nose off-freezes, see I your land's people only in thin blouses and in short socks. How make you it, that you by wind and weather not the humour forlorn goes? Last year to byplay, when I you beseeked and it out all buckets poured, was your comment only short and boundy: Good English weather. Wet till on the bones, found I this not so lusty.

What make you so in this greyfull summer? Day's over is it always only cold, rainrich, total unfriendly. I have shake-frost, and middle in the summer drink I every amount of grog and glow-wine. No weather to lay eggs, muchmore a sow-weather! In this sunbrand-free-zone of the world, where we to home are, falls so much rain, that I already swim-skins between my fingers become.

And then these weather-makers in TV or in the radio. How have I them eaten! They tell me, where the wind blows, what with the clouds loose is, here a Low there a High, but no good outsights. These weather-frogs inform me hair-little, how the weather yesterday was and how it now is – as if I this not self knew. Or is this news perhaps highest interesting and

– 55 –

FREUD UND LEID IM ALLTAG

important for people, who in full-climatized bunkers live or in hermetic off-closed bureaus work and nothing from the outer world withbecome?

And the weather tomorrow? Over the foreoutsay can I me mostly dead-laugh. There is yes my horrorscope by wide exacter. But the official weather-frogs come not from their high horse down. After my understandness of fairplay could they yes say: "Dear people, it does us so sorry, but with our prognosis lay we total wrong yesterday. We had no good day." But they do so, as if nothing were. High-nosy as they are, start they day for day from new, us the blue from heaven to lie. And what have they not all in petto – weather-satellites, weather-watchers in every corner of the world, high-modern computers, and it brings nothing. The weather makes, what it will.

What besays there an old German farmer-rule? When the cock crows on the mist, changes the weather or it remains as it is. This wisdom shall these weather-makers themselves behind the ears write!

And you, my dear Peter, give I still an other value-full tip (in German now: *tipp*), which I from my old friend Helga have: By bad weather must you the sun in your heart carry!

Your true Gisela

Am I now a CallGirl?

DIE GRAUEN ZELLEN DER TELEKOM

Dear Peter,

it gives stories and developments, there can you only with the head shake. A beautifull byplay is the Telekom, which first one pair years exists. Earlier was all peacely united under the hat of the Christel from the Post, also beknown as the good old German Federal Post. But with the time were the people out the telephone-department very un-to-peace. They held themselves longest for what betters than the packet- and letter-carriers, the unproductive foot-folk of the Post.

Ergo was it only follow-right, that a new, separated firm into life called was – the Telekom. And what did these young and very dynamic people as first? The yellow colour was them a thorn in the eye. They said: Yellow stands for letters, packets, the post-horn, when not for the snail-post. But the Telekom is modern, clean and quick.

And what is the ideal symbol-colour for such a noble undertaking, for such a modern, clean and quick firm? You come not thereon: Grey and pink. I know absolute not, why it these two colours be must. But proud as the Telekom is, speaks she from "corporate design".

In this sad and always a bit unappetitely make-up find you now federal-wide these new telephone-cells. Is this perhaps the Telekom's version of "grey cells"?

– 57 –

FREUD UND LEID IM ALLTAG

I wonder me freely, where all the wonder-beautifull yellow cells gone are – perhaps to China?

Grey and pink, pink and grey, what for an image. What for a beautifull street-furniture, what for a berichening for our towns and villages! Overthis find you in many places overhead no off-closed cells more. You telephone practish under free heaven. By wind and weather stand you there, in one hand the hearer, with the other hand hold you the ear to, therewith you what understand can. And then have you no third hand more, what in your organizer after to look, no forth hand for your umbrella. Is this the progress? I say you frank and free: I whistle what on "corporate design"!

But the sharpest piece of the Telekom is new-erthings the bill about my telephone-talks. What me there month for month into the house flatters, mocks of every bewriting. Earlier was on the bill to read: *Ortsgespräche, Ferngespräche, Auslandsgespräche.* This was clip and clear, every little child could it understand. Now find I there: *CityCall, RegioCall, GermanCall* and *GlobalCall.* I think, my good old hamster is ripe for a crisis. What shall so an unsense?

The Telekom has opensightly a bird. It is me and all my friends fullcome unbegriply, which devil these post-modern youngster-designers ridden has. What means *CityCall*, when you not in a city, but on the village live? *GermanCall* is "Deutschruf", but what is a "10 plus Deutschruf"? Comes a *RegioCall* from a handy-besitter out the *InterRegio*? And then the *GlobalCall* – is it a call from the global village or a speaking globe or what?

– 58 –

DIE GRAUEN ZELLEN DER TELEKOM

I know not, where me the head stands. Help, am I now a *CallGirl*?

Your true Gisela

P.S. Now comes a price-question for you: Why only drove Jan Ullrich, the top-sportler of the German Telekom, during the Tour de France in the *yellow* tricot? Likes he also the old telephone-cells more than the new cells?

Britischer geht's nicht

Find you that right?

AN EINEN BERÜHMTEN DETEKTIV

Very honoured Mr. Sherlock Holmes!
You must know, that I so many books from you read
have. I bewonder very your grips and sharp-sense,
with which you all murderers, thieves and swindlers
to the stretch bring. When I me today personly to you
turn, think I, that you the only person of format are,
who me understand and my problem solve can. Even
my friend Peter is of the meaning, that this my fall one
number too great is for our smart Schimanski. Derrick
would still in question come, but he is yes in rest-stand
gone, as also you perhaps withbecome have.

This is my story, hear to: I have two aunts, the Lissy
and the Annie. Aunt Lissy, ifwell already 97 years old,
is still quick-alive. But Aunt Annie, who last November the older of 89 reached, fell newly me nothing you
nothing from the stool and was on the spot mouse-
dead.

While she alone-standing was and always very
sparesome lived has, hinderlets she a gigantic ability:
a house with garden, another ground-piece middle in
the town, costbar jewels, a heap of money and knows
the cuckoo what. Now comes the hammer. Who, think
you, becomes all, this richdom? Only my Cousin Walter, whereagainst I total empty outgo. That find I already very, very markworthy.

Hereto must you the following know. This Walter
came off and to by Aunt Annie foreby, let himself a

– 63 –

BRITISCHER GEHT'S NICHT

cup of coffee inpour and made one on nice conversation. That was all. He falls me simply on the alarm-clock with his slimy art. I thereagainst have often Aunt Annie's socks and undertrousers washed, her dog exported and the table uproomed, when Walter himself already out the dust made had. But this Schicki-Micki is now fine hereout, and I must into the tube look. Find you that right?

The more I over the whole story afterthink, come I to the end, that this Walter the testament falsed has and tofore Aunt Annie what in the coffee done has –with the result, that she much earlier than awaited her spoon offgive and in the grass bite must. Who knows? Man hears and reads yes so allthehand. Every day are newspapers full of horrible stories.

Dear Mr. Sherlock Holmes, you are my last hope. Friendlierwise can you perhaps also your Dr. Watson inswitch, who always for a brilliant idea good is. I go therefrom out, that you this interesting fall overtake can and in your betrued and toforletty art and wise upclear.

I were you so thankbar, when you me some lines tocome let would.

With friendly greetings

Your true Gisela

A *horrible train through the window*

GISELAS ENGLAND-ABENTEUER

Dear Peter,
you will bevoiced know, how it me hewent, after I you
in London good-bye said had. I travelled still three
days through the beutifull landscape of the earl-shaft
Kent. My God, what was I fix and ready, when I from
England tohome came. Bynear all people on board of
the ship were seasick. I could tomindest my *apple-strudel* by me behold. Highest time, that soon the
channel-tunnel comes, therewith all travellers the
overdrive happy overstand can.

But now after the other. Overhead wonder I me,
that it in England not only *apple-strudel*, but also
blackforest gateau, schnaps and *rollmop* gives. Thereby had I such an *angst* (as you say), *angst* before the
English kitchen. And now? All half so bad. I could die
for your puddings. For apple-pie can I all stand and
lie let. Your English tea drink I day and night, on
lovest the Assam. I liked the beefsteak only then not,
when it the quality of an old leather-saddle had. On
the last day was it me too colourfull, and I asked the
upper in the restaurant: *When will I become a soft
steak?* I hope never, said this gentleman, fully cool.
And there was I with my Latin at the end.

How you Englanders the weather so complete ignore can, is me total unbegriply – one of the greatest
riddles of mankind. When it one day's bind-threads
rained and I wet to the bones was, said one man to me

– 65 –

BRITISCHER GEHT'S NICHT

only: Good English weather. I thought, I hear not right! Good English weather. I in my thick winter dress came I me fore like in a cool-cupboard. But your landspeople had no mantle on, no hat, no cap, no shawl, no socks. When I them so naked saw, freezed I still more. No wonder, that nowhere hooks to find are, the clothes up to hang – not in the pub, not in the restaurant, not in the train. I came me so silly fore, when I always forgively after hooks seeked. But this must others be, when you a fullworthy partner in the EG be will – that say I you!

Bed & Breakfast found I fullcome in order. The landladies equal themselves landup, landdown like one egg the other. Only the form of their glasses have adventurous varieties. An adventure is also the opening and closing of these push-windows and the be-serving of the WC. A luck, that the paper in the last years a softer touch accepted has and not more the quality of solid pergament-documents besits. The water for the morning-wash is always ice-cold or so brewing-hot, that you soforth the tea therewith make can. In the last night had I a room, in which it like pike-soup pulled – through the closed window. I could and could not insleep, so cold was it.

What should I the landlord say? I took my German-English wordsbook out the pocket and fumbled this sentences together: *There comes always a horrible train through my window!* The landlord looked me with cow-great eyes on, said but nothing. *Me is so cold, could I please a second ceiling have?* He rolled with his eyes and pulled his brows high. Opensightly thought he, that I not all cups in the cupboard had.

– 66 –

Nothing happened. This shot me through the head: *Wenn der mir nicht eine zweite Decke gibt, will ich hier sofort ausziehen.* But now was this in English over to bring: *When you me not a second ceiling give, will I here soforth undress.*

Knows the shinder, what the landlord understood and from me thought has … On next day made I me on the socks and turned England the back – not for always, hope I.

Your true Gisela

In null comma nothing

INVASION DURCH DEN TUNNEL?

Dear Peter,
luck-wish, heartly luck-wish – now are you Englanders quite stink-normal Europeans! From now on grows together, what since the ice-time parted was. One good day's drive you also not more on the wrong side of the street. No special spleens more. It will end in the total victory of the Continental Breakfast over the Full English Breakfast.

The nail-new Eurotunnel makes it possible. To the opening came extra Elizabeth II. through the tube rushed, total in pink and with a seldom elegant bibi on the head. Against Her Majesty looked Mitterand I. grey in grey out, like the weather. It was a great eye-look, when the two state's upperheads their scissors out the pocket pulled, the band synchron through-cutted and thereto Beethoven's "Song of Joy" he-toned. But why was our Federal Chancellor, the Kohl Helmut, not inloaded, one of the greatest Europeans in the world!? Out-calculated the Mitterand – as European can you him in the pipe smoke. Know you, that he every English word in France forbidden has, even "walkman" and "computer"?! Now are you perplex, what? With right can we us ask, where there the European ghost remains.

For you Englanders is the Eurotunnel opensightly not without problems. Yearhundreds lived you on an isolated island – a little like on the moon. But all eight-

– 68 –

ing. You have you the Armada, Napoleon and Hitler with success from the throat holded. And now this formly inloading to an invasion! But who has an interest? I think, the invaders will your land's people self be, when they in wind's hurry in Calais infall and cheap and much beer buy can.

These modern times. I am sad, that it out and foreby be should, the Sleeve-Channel with the ship to cross. Good, it was me often so bad, that I to die wanted. But then were you always fully de-damaged, when the wonderfull White Cliffs of Dover into the look-field came. And now? You sit in the car, safety-belt on, the car inbedded in a waggon, the waggon inclosed in a tube. A prison-cell is comfortable thereagainst. Underway's see you nothing, hear you nothing – you are not underway's. You travel not to England, suddenly are you there, in null comma nothing.

But for's first is it fullcome unclear, when this new adventure for us normal dying in question comes. Is the yearhundred-buildwerk now ready or not? Goes there all with right things to? My meaning: The tunnel exists in reality overhead not. I saw newly only a film about the opening on TV, a simulation, an alp-dream.

Yes, when it so is: God Save The English Breakfast!
Your true Gisela

Pistol on the breast

AN EINEN BRITISCHEN PREMIER

Dear Mr. John Major,
excusen's me, that I so with the door into *Downing
Street Nr. 10* fall. But what too much is, is too too
much. It goes on no cow-skin – and therewith are we
direct by the theme. Why shall we Germans on devil
come out the beef from your mad cows eat? Thereby
are we yes not so. First shortly had we you the Kohl,
the Chirac and the Klinsmann to visit sent, who abso-
lut beghosted from your beefsteaks and rostbeefs
were. Freely say I you clip and clear: We like the
Tower, but we are not your beefeaters, and first right
not, when the cows BSE have.

But you think well, Mr. Major, that you with us Con-
tinentals make can, what you will. Other folks have
there opensightly more luck. Not a single harsh word
comes over your lips about the Australians, the New
Zealanders or the Americans, who already since 1989
your beef thanking off-lean. Why must alone we your
sins out-bathe? Out which ground is special Germany
such a red cloth for you? Why, dear Mr. Major, must
it now a war on all fronts give? In your newspapers is
to read: The Englanders shall no German beer and no
German wine more drink. How bitter for your folk –
bitter in the truest sense of the word. And why shall
your land's people never, never again BMW or Mer-
cedes drive? Can they this long outhold? Always only
Jaguar and Rolls Royce, me come the tears.

– 70 –

AN EINEN BRITISCHEN PREMIER

How man so hears, are you total sour, that the BBC during the European Football Mastershaft Beethovens's *Song of Joy* as European Hymn played has. Yes, you dear sky! What can the Beethoven therefor? It is not beknown, if he against English beef was. You say, that you Englanders self a row of componists of international format have, who good enough for footballers are. Who then – mean you the Handel perhaps with his music for fire and water-work?

Know you, what in my eyes the greatest scandal is? You, Mr. Major, set us shorterhand the pistol on the breast and hold us in chess: So long we not your beef eat will, runs nothing more in the European Union. Out and foreby. What ever for a problem in Europe on the day's order stands – you say: no, no, no.

My dear Mr. Prime Minister, there must I you into the prayer take: Is this blockade the fine English art? Springs a gentleman so with his friends about? Have you yourself all this right overlaid? Or have you already too much beef from the mad cows eaten?

In deepest sorrow greet I you and hope on an answer.

Your true Gisela

Man makes what through

EG-NORMEN FÜR ENGLAND?

Dear Peter,
in this heavy time, where one problem the other hunts
and where it overall thereunder and thereover goes,
can man glad and happy be, when it a little bit to laugh
gives. But that is it yes, what me sorrows makes. Over
the following story laughs itself half Europe dead,
thewhile you Englanders in this fall no joke understand. Your world-famous humour is you opensightly
total off-hand come.

And this came so: The stone of the kick-off is namely the water-closet, in all world also as WC beknown.
You Englanders can with right proud be, that one of
your land's people this wonderfull thing invented has
– and this already in the Year of the Lord 1596. You
pull the water, and it makes flushshshsh. John Har-
rington out Stepney was the genius, who for the
water-flushing an uncomplicated lifter-system con-
structed, which *without* outrun-ventil outcomes
and quite simple on the under-pressure-principle
berests.

On the European Continent thereagainst, where
the WC two-hundred years later quasi new invented
was, dominates since people's memory the water-
flushing *with* an outrun-ventil. This system is until
today in the United Kingdom forbidden. Continental
producers of water-flush-boxes have not the breath of
a chance on the English market. Quite clear is this a

– 72 –

EG-NORMEN FÜR ENGLAND?

heavy sin against the European ghost and the open market – all what right is!

Otherside's must man you Englanders a bit in protection take. Through practical tests and experiments was halt outfound, that the English water-boxes much better their service do than the Continental water-boxes. You have please-nice understandness, that I you not all the details up-table. Only so much: The Continental glide-effect lets very to wish over.

And this can fortrue not shit-equal be. You British say: One of our culture-goods is in highest danger! Alone the beforestanding import of the German toilet-bowl must a catastrophe in your eyes be. Where you British only deep-flush toilet-bowls know, have we Germans mostest flat-flush bowls. I ask you: What is better, before you the water pull – to inspect or not to inspect? That is here the question.

May be, that for this problem-fall a compromise in sight is. But how man so hears, remains your Director of the BBC (British Bathroom Council) absolute hard in the question of the water-box: "We in England had already perfect water-closets, when the Continental brothers and sisters still on their thunder-balks and plop-latrines sat. Why shall we a minder-worthy system into our land let?" No wonder, that him the laugh forgone is.

Me would interest, by the way: Exist also regulations for the (we say: *Klobrillen*) toilet-glasses? Man makes what through.

Your true Gisela

– 73 –

From woman to woman

GISELA FASST SICH EIN HERZ

Dear Queen Elizabeth!
Tofirst would I you in German write, while my English not form the finest is, think I. And there fell me in, what I newly in the wait-room of my tooth-doctor read had: Your royal better half, the Prince Philipp, can himself quite good in German toright find. But then thougth I: silly sense! What have you from a letter in German, when your man not tohome is and himself liver in the world-history about-drives –playing polo or looking after wild animals? Were it there not better to have a direct wire from woman to woman, or?

It can be, that you yourself already the whole time wonder, why you a letter from a Gisela out Germany in your royal hands hold. The ground is the following: I and my friends make us great sorrows about your oldest son, the Charles. Can man him still as a thrownfollower besign?

We are great fans of the English Kingshouse, but this must once said be: We think, it is not good, that Charles, who king learned has, job's loose is and that already over so many years now. That can not good go. It is fore all not god for the together-living with the poor Di, who it all outbathe must, when the Charles days-long not so good thereupon is.

Can your highness yourself not a royal push give and the thrown for your son free-make? As with-feeling

– 74 –

mother must you the royal heart bleed, when you with onsee must, that your Charles himself in such an outsight's loose situation befinds. How long shall this then still so further go? Till you 80 are? Or 90? Or 100? I ask you in full earnest: Is it a perspective for a dynamic man like he, who so on wire is – only on the day to wait, that his mother the royal spoon off-gives? He has grey hairs already, while I not one single grey hair on your royal overhead see.

There help no pills and no cold envelopes: Such frust leads unupholdsome to newroses, from which the world so full is in these days. Can you this with onsee, when it itself thereby about your own flesh and blood handles? Nothing for ungood. But can you, worthy Queen, not an elegant way find off to thank and apple and sceptre to your royal aftergrow to over-reach? And that were no shame. Think only of your royal colleague, Queen Juliane from the Netherlands, who herself right-time to rest set and her daughter further-govern let – and that in an older, when Beatrix what therefrom had. Safely can you so what after-feel – special you, who as a still blood-young thing to the thrown came.

And can you not fallen find to the thought, that you yourself back-pull? Let it slow go, read a good book and play with your lovely ankles! Were that nothing? And the Charles as lucky king! I think, you overlay you that, I feel it already. It were too beautifull, from you to hear.

Your true butler, your he-giving

Gisela Daum

BUCKINGHAM PALACE

24th June, 1988.

Dear Miss Daum,

    I am commanded by The Queen to acknowledge your letter of 11th June and to say that the views you express in it about The Prince of Wales have been noted.

    Since there is no question of Her Majesty abdicating the Throne, there is no comment to be made on this subject.

                Yours sincerely,

                (ROBERT FELLOWES)

Gun by foot

DIE SORGE UM DEN THRONFOLGER

Greet God, Queen Elizabeth!
Sorry, that I so with the door into the house fall.
Queens gives it yes enough. But we forget all too easy,
that kings outdie like seldom insects or seldom flowers. When that so wider goes, gives it over short or
long only these four kings: Cross, Pike, Heart and
Karo King. There must unbethinged what done be,
but what?

Fall's you now the roast smell, can I you clear wine
inpresent. It is too good beknown – no, I will this with
you discuss: Your Majesty thinks not the bean thereon, back to step and the thrown for Prince Charles to
room, the designed after-follower. Yes, you will your
grounds have, all what right is.

But me bleeds the heart, Charly's hair with the years
greyer and greyer to see and his royal face longer and
longer. It cries to the sky, how lost and lonely the
crown-prince middlerwhile out the washing looks.
And what was he once for a much-promising, life's
lusty young man! Newerthings is he so total down,
that he always only the architects and planners what
on the roof gives. Freely have I also what against their
ice-blocks and the whole shit, which they – also here
in Munich – together-build and then "postmodern"
call.

But the Charles goes much too wide in this fall. The
architects are not the sin-bucks for all evil in the

– 77 –

world. They are much more handlongers of our glory-rich society, to which we all gohear. See you, there drift we quite beautifull from the theme off. The theme is: How can we the prince happier make?

I think, I have found the poodle's kernel, sotosay the stone of the wise. My Aunt Lissy and even Cousin Walter (who always a hair in the soup find) are full beghosted from this my idea: Prince Charles should King of Germany become! What hold you therefrom? All your problems and all his problems would be loosened with one beat. And here in this our land stands a whole folk gun by foot to begreet the Charly as the new state-overhead: Hail you in the victory-kranz! There had we, what we always wanted. How unendly good were this for our selfworth-feeling. For a monarchy in Germany would our Federal President even with pleasure soforth in rent go.

My infall is overhead not out the air gripped, when your and our history you what says. Twohundred years back were *we* it namely, who you with the Georges out Hanover as kings outhelped! Why not *vice versa* now? The new residence for Charles must yes not in Hanover be, with all the rummel of the Expo 2000. We should over Munich as a residence afterthink.

Everyfalls go I stark therefrom out, that Your Majesty me a well-willing letter tocome let will.

Your true butler

Gisela Daum

BUCKINGHAM PALACE

8th September, 1989.

Dear Miss Daum.

The Queen has commanded me to thank you for your letter of 23rd August.

It was kind of you to have written, but I can assure you that there is no chance of The Prince of Wales becoming King of Germany.

Yours sincerely

(ROBERT FELLOWES)

Miss G. Daum.

I and the Queen

ALS DAS WÜNSCHEN NOCH GEHOLFEN HAT

Dear Peter,
what think you, when our Federal President or myways also the Federal Chancellor one day's their private rooms wide open would? Put you so what fore:
Hinz and Kunz snuffle in all corners about, make
themselves over the pictures on the wall lusty, be-
trample with their dirty shoes the costbar carpets and
hinderlet the toilet in a tostand, which to heaven
stinks. Not out to paint! I every fall's would this not
tolet. Not for money and good words.

But what shall's. Shortly had your Queen the fantastic infall, the Buckingham Palace for visitors up to
close. And people out all gentlemen's lands followed
the royal call in masses. For tourists is it naturely a
found eating. Who five times by Madame Tussaud was
or already the Londoner Zoo beseeked has, is it a nice
off-change, in the royal roomlinesses to lust-wandle.
Fore all is it a good alternative idea, when it – how so
often in London – in streams rains.

And when in the entrance-price not only a look on
the royal stamp-collection inbegripped is, but also a
little cup tea with Her Majesty, would the luck fullcome be. What for a vision, no, it can tomorrow reality be: I and the Queen – we two together – take a
flowery Assam or an elegant Darjeeling to us! Or
stands she on a characterfull Ceylon, who knows? On
each fall would the Queen beghosted be, how I the

– 80 –

ALS DAS WÜNSCHEN NOCH GEHOLFEN HAT

tea-cup hold, with the little finger outstretched namely. Very cultivated, naturely. And when she good
thereupon is, would she muchlight say: "Gisela, you
should Elizabeth to me say."

This all can you self-speaking not gratis have. The
Queen opens the Palace not because of your blue
eyes. This understands every little child. Her Majesty
wishes pinke-pinke to see, moses and the prophets,
cash (as we in German say). We must bethink, for
what she not all money outgive must! Alone the many
hats and uncounted shoes, the dogs and the horses,
and all the servants and lackeys.

And one unluck comes seldom alone. How it the
devil will, is newly also still the Windsor Palace off-
burnt. This will all bepayed be. From nothing comes
nothing.

What teaches us this here in Germany? When the
state the bread-basket higher hangs and we all us in-
cupboard must, is not only the little man asked, but
also the high animals. That has the Queen good made!
I will soforth a letter to our Federal President write.
He could also his private chambers for the publicity
upmake and with the entrance-money of the people a
good purpose under the arms grip!

What hold you from my idea?

Your true Gisela

Bethink it, oh soul!

AN EINEN BUCHCLUB IN ENGLAND

Very honoured Madams and Sirs,
you have me shortly a prospect in the house flatter let
with a wonderfull idea: *Any three English books for
only 5 DM.* Too lovesworthy of you – but I am overhead not safe, if I the right person am, in you book-
club intostep. I know not, if I enough English on the
box for so what have.Must man/woman the Abitur
forewise or tomindest the middle ripeness? Or is my
English so or so outreaching for your standard?

One must I you but say: I will not the books in my
book-cupboard for decoration put. Such books are
there already toheap partly bound in swine's leather
and with goldcut. What I want, is a really good book
in English to read. But I can not simply over my shad-
ow jump. Perhaps can you me with council and deed
to side stand.

Othersides will I not under the carpet sweep, that I
me so my own thoughts over your program make. To
byplay is me upfallen: The book *1984* is total olded.
Can you please the author the hot tip give, that he his
book actualizes? A simple look on the calendar would
already outreaching be. And then the memories of
Roger Vadim. Think you, that the German house-
women nothing better to do have than from his hich-
hack betouched to be, which he with such wife's pictures like the Bardot, the Deneuve or the Fonda had?

Beyond from good and bad is well your *History of*

– 82 –

AN EINEN BUCHCLUB IN ENGLAND

England or the work *Castles and Horses in Britain* –
but why must it castles and horses be? Are these books
full of peace, joy, egg-cake? I must freely say, that I
stark forebeholds have againstover so off-kicking ti-
tles like *Sex Watching* , *Nude Photography* and *Lady
Chatterley's Lover*.

Bethink it, oh soul! What you so from the moral of
a throughcutly German man or woman hold, lets yes
deep look. Such indecent books under our folk to
bring! Is their inhold perhaps cleaner and onstandier
in English?

And before I it forget: I wonder me total, that you
not one single book from the Shakespeare William on
the list have. Is this classical champignon not more so
in? That would I very, very sad find – where I his *Mid-
summernight's Dream* so much like – special in the
version of the fantastic Woody Allen.

With friendly greetings

Gisela Daum

Total on the woodway

DEUTSCHE SPRACHE, SCHWERE SPRACHE?

Dear Peter,
when you me in next time beseek come, overlay I now already, how you here in Germany toright come will. Highest important is it, always and overall a good impression to make. Thereto can you often this hear: Dresses make people. But I think, with this onsight lie you today to day mostest wrong. Thathalf say I lover: Speech makes people. It is important, what out your mouth comes.

Many Englanders think yes: German speech – heavy speech. But I say you: Nothing is lighter, than the German speech to speak. The deeper ground for this? We have tenthousands of words in our both speeches, which total the same are: *finger, ring, hand, arm, bus, wind, pudding.* Then comes the great mass of words, where only a very little difference to see is: *nose, hair, breast, apple, shoe.* One good day's should it a German-English commission give, which out these words the same in both speeches makes. The school-children will us on eternal times thankbar be.

When you not safe are, try a German outspeak of English words. In the most falls claps it like smeared. Here is a little overlookable list for the begin: *communication, information, system, project, innovation, offensive.* The people here think, that you very educated or tomindest fashionable are – special when it self about readers of the *Zeit* or the *Süddeutsche* han-

– 84 –

DEUTSCHE SPRACHE, SCHWERE SPRACHE?

dles. Next step: Take three of these words and all your courage together and say to byplay: *kommunikatives Informations-System* or *projektierte Innovations-Offensive*. These international plastic-words help you very much for the begin.

One great request have I freely at you: Please overset *not* the following words – you come in devil's kitchen. The Germans would you overhead not understand. They are namely hundred percent therefrom overclothed, that these words original to the German word-treasure belong: *programme, connection, cool, download, reader, easy, knowhow, container, recycling, t-shirt, second hand, mega-out, feeling, timing, last not least, ladies first* and many others more. Bind some of these words loose together, to byplay: *Über welche Connection kann ich dieses coole Programm downloaden? Ist der Reader easy oder brauche ich etwas Knowhow? In welchem Container kann ich dieses T-Sirt, das nur second hand war und nun mega-out ist, recyceln?* Or try it with this set: *Last not least, du hast kein Feeling für das richtige Timing!* Every German person is soforth in the picture. No pig here would on the idea come, that you an outlander are. And this is heretolands so good like a life-assurance.

You must know: We Germans like the English speech over all measures. We invent even English words, when you Englanders the fantasy outgoes and you not know, how many expressions formly in the air lie. One good byplay is "oldtimer" for an old car. You know this overhead not and like to speak of a "veteran car". Still better is the "handy", which here in all

– 85 –

BRITISCHER GEHT'S NICHT

mouths is, but which you only as "mobile telephone" beknown is. But is not "handy" the best word for this wonderfull new thing? Is it not much nearer at the pulse of time?

But I will you one warning still with on the way give. Please forseek not, too much German to speak. These Germans overfall you solikeso with the English language (or what they therefor hold), so that you absolute no chance have. But say them always, that their English astonishingly good is – even if they only so with the German "r" roll or no "th" over the tongue bring. Everybody likes to hear this, also when it a fist-thick lie is. But what says my Aunt Lissy? A nice lie is like a nice ornament.

And when you with me to my aunt's birthday-party go, sing you please *not*, what you in *your* German lessons learned have: *Zum Geburtstag viel Glück!* This can you forget, there are you total on the woodway. The melody is the self, but land up, land down sing we quite simple: "Happy birthday to you!" This can you even in our children's garden hear, but here clings it so: *Hebt die Bürste, juhu!*

Your true Gisela

– 86 –

Deutsches Wesen und die Welt

Order must be!

„DIN" GEHT ÜBER ALLES

Dear Peter,
newly was I with the car in the town to besorrow me
this and that for the holidays. Opensigthly had many
people this wonderbat idea. The town was namely
pickpack full and no park-place in sight. I drove three
rounds round th blocks. Endly – with cooking motor
– had I unhomely luck.

The horsefoot thereby was only, that I a park-disc
needed. I knew it quite exact, I had a disc from the
circle-spare-cashbox last year, but where was that silly
thing? I put the whole car total on the head, and this
came to the fore-shine: a lipstick and an off-broken
comb, a long-seeked theatre-ticket and an ice-
scratcher, a dirty bullet-writer and a town-plan from
1978 – but no park-disc.

What do, spoke Zeus? I pulled simply a piece paper
out my bag, wrote "Arriving 15:30 clock" on it and let
it sightbar behind the window in the car lie. Clever,
not true?

But know you, what loose was, when I from the
shopping to my drivable under-sentence back came –
full bepacked and fullcome outer breath? There stood
a policeman and wrote already my number up. Said
this friend and helper to me: That makes 20 marks for-
waring's money, please-nice. I think, I hear not right.
I was like from thunder beaten. It gives moments,
there can you not more, there break you together.

– 89 –

DEUTSCHES WESEN UND DIE WELT

And my notice "Arriving 15:30 clock"? Forget it.
That could he on no fall accept, gave he to understand, that was against all fore-scripts – no, no, no.
And then held he me an evening-filling speech, which
very impression's full was: An orderly German park-
disc must 15 cm high be and 11 cm broad, no millimetre more and no millimetre less. The number and
the bookstables on it must from DIN 1451, part 2, be
taken – when you this what says. As colour comes only
park-blue (what else?) in question, strict after DIN
6171. And woe, you let yourself what others infall, so
like I with my hand-written notice. There could yes
every body come. Yes, where are we then?

That ask I me allthethings now also. Is it not wonderbar, that we no greater problems in this our republic have? Is it not to deepest bequieting, that heretolands on every little thing thought is?

I tell you what: Over short or long must even the wc-
paper normed be, DIN A6 from next year on. Shit
what thereupon.

Your true Gisela

The yellow from the egg

DEUTSCHE GEMÜTLICHKEIT

Dear Peter,

when you through our old German towns walk, befalls you sometimes a strong feeling – the feeling of *Heimat* and *Gemütlichkeit*. An oversetting is heavy, and I think, these German words are you beknown and speak for themselves. Americans and Japanese come yes extra over the great pond to seek this nostalgic feeling here. They bathe then in this fantastic feeling after heart's lust, while the towns in their homelands only out louder quick-streets and cloud-scrapers bestand.

Not gratis spoke I from walking or going to foot. Then when first the cars into the old-towns infall, is it out and foreby with the *Gemütlichkeit*. There is a noise and a stinking, that you the legs under the arm take and quickly the wide seek. Horrible, how many people round and round drive and this hourslong, only a parkplace to seek. And when they not a place for their drivable undersentence find can, make they it often on the criminal tour: park in the second row, before an outdrive or just in the footganger-zone, where the people then round about these benzine-boxes slalom run must.

And exact there have the town-fathers and town-planners a new philosophy developed, the cars from the people away to keep – posts and pollers. Our German towns are now full of them: posts in thick and

– 91 –

DEUTSCHES WESEN UND DIE WELT

thin, posts out metal, wood or plastic, posts in modern
and in old-modern look (as we in German say) – sometimes bandaged with beautifull chains. Upperest aim
is – what always that means – the bettering of the
quality of the street-room. But in reality is it so: The
posts can very easy overseen be. And then run you
with full steam against them, mostly with the most
sensible parts of your body. Still badder is it, when you
this with the bicycle passes: throat- and leg-break!

The pollers are a bit more representative and not so
easy to oversee. Footgangers have no problems with
them, but the cars. While it not heavy is, a post with a
car flat to lay, makes a poller rulemassy a bump in your
car. The ground: Pollers are very massive, mostly out
beton. You can a large tankship on them rope. Germany has yes so many harbour-towns. A little friendlier are the smaller, half-round pollers – in every rela-
tion the yellow from the egg. And no town can in face
of this development behind-stand. So have they Munich and Würzburg total be-pollered, Tübingen and
Heidelberg, Gütersloh and Castrop-Rauxel. Even on
our smallest villages can you posts and pollers find.

But with posts and pollers is it longest not done.
Town-planners think day and night thereover after,
how they their town what good do can. The street-
room cries after street-furniture. You have no idea, on
what the German invention's ghost else still come can:
all sorts of boxes and bowls, round, square or with
three corners. But the pride of the town-fathers are
these gigantic flower-bowls in form of six-corner-
mothers. They are out beton and see really not nice
out. But when they with stepmothers or geraniums

– 92 –

DEUTSCHE GEMÜTLICHKEIT

beplanted are, comes soforth this bescribed feeling of *Heimat* and *Gemütlichkeit* high.

And a bank out thick mesh-wire with a paper-basket on the side or one of these unupfalling bicycle-standers complete the street-furniture, give the street-room the rest.

How expresses it one of your greatest poets so right: The rest is silence.

Your true Gisela

I am not an outlander!

DIE DEUTSCHEN ALS GEBORENE INLÄNDER

Dear Peter,
newerthing's have we Germans one big problem. No,
it is not the question, who the next Federal Chancellor or the next Federal President be will. The problem
number one is also not, if we themnext the World-
master or the European Footballmaster make or not.
Little fishes. I will you not longer on the folter span:
All world is of the meaning, that we Germans a hate
on all outlanders have.

I think, that the antipart the fall is. We love the outlanders formly and have them in our heart closed – to
byplay Rudi Carrell, Erika Berger, the Simpsons,
Howard Chippendale and many, many more. Our
loveling's outlanders are to time the Japanese. Out the
whole mass can I here freely only one pair uplist –
Toyota and Mitsubishi, Hitachi and Sony, Yamaha and
Kawasaki, Yashica and Minolta, Seiko and Fuji. And
then eat we in our own land bynear only outlandish –
Pizza, Lasagne, Cheeseburger, Paella, Nasi Goreng,
Cevapcici, Smörrebröd, Gyros and Kebab. I ask you:
Where is there the outlander-hate?

Or throw a look on our bestseller-lists of books:
Outer the Walser Martin and the Drewermann Eugen
find you wide and broad there no inhomish poets! Our
babies carry not more so old-German names like Günter, Werner, Dieter, Marlies, Ingrid or Gisela. They
hear on names like Mika, Jarne, Yannick, Shirelle,

DIE DEUTSCHEN ALS GEBORENE INLÄNDER

Chantal or Suleika. No, that let we us not aftersay, that we no heart for the outlanders have! And when in Hoyerswerda and otherswhere here and there one pair stones fly, then is this a shame, but not typical. There is the through-look lost gone. We have absolute nothing against outlanders.

But what we in the soul not outstand can, is poor to be. That have the most of us behind us. That will we not more. There must also the outlanders an insee have. When they money withbring and with us shops make, will we the last be, them to hate. But when they as poor swallowers come, our jobs in danger bring, with our girls flirt and us the butter from bread take, then are we with right sour. Why give we then so richly for *Misereor* or *Bread for the World*? That the poor church-mouses remain, where they are. This is a clear world-order, understand you?

We have no problems with outlanders. Highest go they us the on the nerves, when they overhand take. There read I in every newspaper and on every litfaß-column: "I am an outlander!" And that say people, from whom you never thought had, that they outlanders are – Thomas Godschalk and Witta Pohl, Steffi Graf and Günther Jauch, Uli Hoeneß and the Breitner Paul! What shall this coming-out? When that so wider goes, is also Heino an outlander – or perhaps Carolin Reiber, Berti Vogts, Dr. Oetker and the Wildecker Heartboys?

Thereby are we Germans absolute no outlanders, we are the born inlanders. And the outland respects this. Where always on the world we our holidays make, become we our *Eisbein mit Sauerkraut*, our

– 95 –

DEUTSCHES WESEN UND DIE WELT

Knödel and *Strudel* served, thereto our good German filter-coffee with the *Verwöhnaroma*. This comic feeling, an outlander to be, know we overhead not. Not even, when we us in the outland befind.

Your true Gisela

P.S. We are yes not so, we let us always what infall. Exclusive for poor outlanders put we heretolands now containers up, so that they therein live could – longest not so uncomfortable like the containers for glass and paper. And the addresses are from finest – today the exquisite Theresien Meadow, tomorrow the English Garden and the Mary Place. Is that perhaps nothing?

After us the sin-flood

WO IST DIE MAUER?

Dear Peter,
what are five years, what are ten years? A long time, a short time? So without wider's can you that not say. I give you a byplay: When I from time to time to Berlin come, go me formly the eyes over. So many new build-projects on one heap can you not still once in the whole world see. Houses shoot like mushrooms out the soil. The result is a nice new world.

And then goes me through the head: How was it earlier here? All is so fullcome others. Five years already reached total out, that you no memory more have – like a *blackout*, as we in German say. I make a bummel through Cross-mountain and know me not more in and out. And with me make dozens of tourists out all gentlemen's lands the self experience. They hold a map in the hand and have complete the orientation lost. Where stood the Wall, where only?

In only five mouths was 1991 the most of the 43 kilometre "anti-imperialistic protection-wall" off-roomed. Many parts were sold or presented, some were stolen. My Cousin Walter made himself extra on the way, a piece of the beton ownhandy out the Wall to pick. Like Walter have now uncounted masses of land's people a little fragment of the Wall to home in the vitrine. A million ton of the buildwork was granulated for the building of new streets between east and west. Very symbolic – but is this enough?

DEUTSCHES WESEN UND DIE WELT

I can it yes understand, that fore all the people out the east the snout full had from the Wall and it not more to see wanted. Away with it! Middlerwhile can you parts of the Wall in Israel, London, Mexico, Riga, Moscow, Prag, Los Angeles and who knows where bewonder, but so good like nothing in Berlin. I ask you: Is this the right way? Must we not also such a hated symbol beware and from it learn? What shall the afterworld from us say? I tell you, what *we* today say: After us the sin-flood.

But I can me therewith not off-find. How hold we it with the memory? Shall we so do, as if it the Wall never given had? Are the Germans a folk of Alzheimers? Only very, very little rests of the Wall are saved. And when we not up-pass, will also these overremainsels one day's over the Jordan go.

Only some people make themselves a pair thoughts. The latest cry is the project of a seven centimetres broad copper-band along the line, where the Wall through Berlin ran. Or, if this too costbar is, a blue-red double band out beton.

How also ever, sponsors are heartly welcome. I see already the shield from Coca Cola: Here stood the Wall from 1961 to 1989 ... *can't beat the feeling!*

Your true Gisela

A *devil will I do!*

DEUTSCHE RECHTSCHREIBREFORM

Dear Peter,
what think you are in moment the greatest problems
here in Germany? That millions of people no job
have? Here the rich Wessies and there poor Eassies?
That the rents and pension not safe are? I say you cliff
and clear: All wrong! We know to time no bigger
theme than the sonamed right-write-reform.

Good, what and how we Germans so write, has
withunder no hand and no foot: "blau", but "rauh";
"Auto fahren", but "radfahren"; "Pappplakat", but
"Schiffahrt". There finds no pig through. And you as
outlander, who German learns, must the hat high go.
Without the Duden under the arm come you practish
not more out. But we have yes sixteen culture-ministers, who day and night besorrowed are, that it us
good goes and that the life not too hard is. What shall
we in future little write, what great? What must we together-write, what outanother? Must there a comma
before "and" stand or not? How shall we a word part,
when the line to end is? You see, questions over questions.

After a yearslong hickhack and many crazy discussion before and behind the stage have now the culture-ministers in their unendly goodness befound:
Newerthings shall we "Zu-cker" write, but not "Mu-
tter". "Meis-ter" is now correct and also "Isos-tasie".
This understand, who will. The reformers have still

– 99 –

DEUTSCHES WESEN UND DIE WELT

more crazy things in petto: "ext-ra", but "Ex-trakt". "Fotografie" shall o.k. be, but not "Filosofie". The "Rhabarber" must the "h" behold, but not the "Delphin", the "Thunfisch" or the "Känguruh". Out "Stengel" is now "Stängel", but out "setzen" not "sätzen". But all our books must for this snick-snack new printed be. What a yearhundred-work be should, is complete into the trousers gone.

No wonder, that on ground of such a little-caro nonsense a protest-storm over the land swept. Our poets and thinkers gave out deepest heart to protest: No, not with us! They have also our Federal President on their side, who mostest the nail on the head hits. And the culture-ministers? They will absolute not from their high horse down-come. They say simple: Ätsch (speak: age), it is now too late! The poets – please nice – could write, how they like. Overhead is the reform only for schools and public offices thought.

Only for schools and offices? I think, I hear not right! What can the poor children therefore, that the culture-ministers nothing better's infalls? And what shall out all the others become, all the Otto Normal Consumers? Who thinks, that I the reform blindlings befollow will, has himself orderly in the finger cut. A devil will I do!

Your true Gisela

– 100 –

You dear sky!

DER GARTENZWERG ALS KULTURGUT

Dear Peter,

a house can still so nice from the architect designed be, the real crowning of a house is a garden. A garden lets the house like a jewel into the eye spring. But know you, what the crowning of a garden is? It is not the pond with the gold-fishes, it is not the Hollywood-swing, not the finest English grass, it are not the nicest roses. As absolute high-point comes only the garden-gnome in question, who the luck fullcome makes. There speak I many people out the soul.

The garden-gnome is out the German, yes the European culture-scene mot more away to think. In export are we Germans the greatest, but what the import of garden-gnomes onbelongs, are we more to-back-holding, not to say: a bit own and restrictive. As to byplay the gnome out Poland with the norm of the German garden-gnome not with-hold can, allow we the Polish gnome not, over the Oder-Neiße-line into our land to come. With right are the Polish gnome-producers stink-sour. But norm is norm, there has even the EG an eye on. How also always, world-wide seen, is the garden-gnome popular and prominent.

Thereby had these neatly creatures earlier heavy times through to make. It gives namely not only the absolute love-havers of garden-gnomes, but also absolute haters, whom these unguilty little men in the flower-beet a thorn in the eye are. These haters had

DEUTSCHES WESEN UND DIE WELT

nothing others to do, than to the kadi to run. They could it soulish not outhold, gave they to understand, that they day for day such an ugly monster to face become must.

Thathalf were these haters of the meaning: Garden-gomes should per law strict forbidden be, basta. But there were these culture-banauses total on the wood-way. They became not right. The highest kadis in this our land had a heart for the the little men. They lifted the garden-gnomes sotosay into the rank of an evening-landish culture-good. Right so!

And when it first so wide come is, can you for nothing more guarantee. The garden-gnome is not simply a culture-good, he can a work of highest art be. And as such come the gnomes in all forms, colours and greats into the trade. Twenty million exemplars stand alone in our German gardens – one nicer than the other. The real garden-gnome is of course out solid ceramic made, about god's will not out cheap plastic.

While I so from criminal stories beghosted am, is my absolute favourite the murdered gnome with the knife in the back. Some real red blood dripples also out his body. He has an honour-place in my fore-garden. But special this type of a gnome is again a stone of the off-kick. Know you, what my neighbour newly to me said? I should me what shame, such a greysome fore-picture for the children off to give. You dear sky! In what for a land live we then? I mean, who not even a little bit black humour off can, should not formly his eye on such a poor garden-gnome throw – or? Problems have the people.

Your true Gisela

– 102 –

DER GARTENZWERG ALS KULTURGUT

P.S. It gives me freely very to think, that I wide and broad no *woman* as garden-gnome seen have. Where remains there the justification? Where is there the equal-berighting after the ground-law?

We are again who

DANK DAIMLER UND DANK GUILDO

Dear Peter,

all world speaks therefrom, that Germany in a deep crisis is. Bynear five million time-companions can absolute no job find. Sad, sad. Where are the "bloomimg landscapes", which our Chancellor with full mouth for the eastly fatherland promised has? Our schools and universities have no world-call more, highest help-school standard. What man there learns, is for nothing good – for today not and for tomorrow first right not. Out international sight are we there only in the underest middle-field to find. Our kids sit day and night before the goggle-box. No wonder, that they the purest criminals are.

Short and good, we Germans – we as eternal world-masters on all fields – are total on the dog come. But such a negative label will our Federal President not on his folk sit let. He preaches landup, landdown: Germany has the whole world shown, what a *rucksack* is; now must a *ruck* through this our nation go.

What-always this means. I have overlayed and over-layed, how I you this idea clear make could. But what shall I say: In-between *is* a ruck through our land gone. And not only one single ruck, it came much-more an earth-quake equal. First overrushing: The right-extremists die not out. We find by us more brown sauce than man think can. The DVU namely came out the stand with nearto thirteen percent into

DANK DAIMLER UND DANK GUILDO

the land-day of Saxonia-Onhold. This is a result, of which the Greens and the Free Democrates only dream can. They remained under five percent. When this not a ruck is and what for a one!

Now comes the second ruck: The Daimler and the Chrysler go together. It is the absolute hammer. Two elephants in one bed, goes this with right things to? The folk's mouth has everyfall's the right answer: "Crime-ler". But what shall's. It is now before all eyes clear, that we Germans no longer the poor sausages of the world-trade are. With the globalization can we throughout withhold, but hallo. The springing point is money, money, money – Germoney.

But the third ruck is the greatest: Guildo Horn. You know him since Birmingham. It is sensational, how he our hearts in storm conquered has. He is not just a singer, but a cult-figure, the "Master" even. Guildo Horn stands for the inner voice in each of us, which says: Do exact that, after which you the sense stands. Just do it. Guildo lives it out – the true and filled life. Call it "authentic". By this new philosophy need you not much after-thinking. It goes only about nut-corners and himberry-ice. And: Guildo has you love – peep, peep, peep.

Now will I close. You must yourself over us Germans no sorrows make. It goes us good. The German crisis exploded like soap-bubble. Forget the DVU. Daimler and Master Guildo have us saved. The message is: We are again who.

Your true Gisela

With four boys is it easy

WIE GEHT EIGENTLICH SKAT?

Dear Peter,
heartly thank for your nice explanation of the menstruations of cricket. After like before have I so my problems with the understanding of your folk's sport nummer one. But today will I me revenge with the menstruations of our beloved cardplay with the name Skat.

This true-German play is from three players gambled. By four players must always the player outset, who just the cards outgives. This is not so bad, while this the chance is, to the WC to go or new beer to fetch or both. All the things are the most players very angry, when the fourth man by all players to kiebitz starts, while he longwhile has. Kiebitzing is not so very wanted.

You need 32 cards. After a good mixture, but not too long, becomes everyman ten cards, two go into the stick. In Hamburg has a man himself newly deadmixed. Then look you your cards on. Now is it quite, quite important, which of the four boys or farmers you have – *with* one plays two, with two plays three and so wider and so forth. But you must no sorrows have: *Without* one plays also two. How also ever – this factor multiply you with the colour, which you to play want. It is 9 for caro (or the hens' dog), 10 for heart, 11 for pike, 12 for cross. When you a half way's good leaf have, can you 18 say. And it goes it this row-fol-

– 106 –

low: Give, hear, say. My Cousin Walter says always 18, also when he absolute nothing to order has. When the others also what on the hand have, say they 20, 22, 23, 24, 27 and so wider – till all away are and one the play becomes.

Now comes it: He can look into the stick and two cards away-press, which he not use can. He says also on, which colour triumph is. When a card out-played is, must you it serve. When you not serve can, can you prick or a card off-throw. So go the pricks round, till you no card more on the hand have. Then are the pricks counted. You must 61 eyes have to win the game against the others. With 61 is it split-arse and a great pitch. When you under 30 eyes have, are you tailor. When you say and write nothing become have, are you tailor-black.

What you perhaps not so democratic find, is that always two against one play. But so is it often in life, and like in the real life hangs it now therefrom off, what tricks you know to overlive. One important menstruations is to byplay: Long way – long colour, short way – short colour. Or: King in the third gives always a prick.

When you too much time for you overlaying need, ask the others often: Which colour play we now? Or they say in this situation also: Card or a piece wood. On best is it, when you many farmers have. I say you: With four boys is it easy. Then can you grand-hand play and them tailor-black make. But this is it, what the others overhead not like. When you your triumph so right outcost will, say the comrades only: great-mother-play.

DEUTSCHES WESEN UND DIE WELT

Before I it forget: Naturely can you also nil play or an open nil – you Englanders say "love" in tennis. But back to our Skat. When you an open nil play, say the others soforth: Trousers down! And when you then the wrong lady pressed have – I say you –, then look you very, very old out.

When you soon to Germany come, can you safely this lusty game with us play. What for a fun will we have!

Your true Gisela

Self is the man

EIN VOLK VON HEIMWERKERN

Dear Peter,

opensightly are we Germans no lazy folk. When I me so round look in this our land, spring me louder active and dynamic people in the eye. They make jogging, when they from the work come, play tennis or have some other sweat-driving sport as hobby. Late evening's are they always still fit like a turn-shoe. How comes this? I tell you the ground: Mindest three of four workers are with only one job longest not outgolasted.

No wonder, that blackwork "in" is. Who blackwork not so bitter needy has, lays freely not the hands in the lap, he finds work enough in his home. Such people name we in German: "homeworkers". These species of time-companions works every thing short and little, what them in the hands falls. And they can no end find. Their houses and cellars are a life's long build-place. Sotosay a fight-place for all the machines and tools, which a true homeworker in his besit and under control has.

Out economic and psychologic sight is the home-workelei fully o.k., it can a heap money spare and gives you the wonderbar feeling of "Self is the man" (or the woman, if you so will). What in us is, must somehow out into the world. Who knows, what we there off-work with the borer in the hand? Many individuals follow the slogan: Through *Bosch* to the only

DEUTSCHES WESEN UND DIE WELT

true I. The chalk-sand-stone of the ownhome makes yes all with – self when the wall through-holed is like Swiss cheese. Overhead the borer. The build-markets say, that on every German middlerwhile mindest three bore-machines fall. And an end of the borer-boom is not in sight.

But some homeworkers have wider-going ambitions. While the learned hand-workers rare and expensive are, lay millions of Germans overall self hand on. They hammer, nail, saw and are top experts in wood. Whole hordes of with-burgers polish and paint and lay carpets out. A right homeworker can golden toilets inbuild and bathrooms from finest. Little fishes. He is instand, his home quite alone high to pull – perfect from the cellar to the roof, with all chicanes.

And the end from the song? The ideal homeworker is also his own architect, who his house not on the paper, but complete in his head has. Little problems are there not the speech's worth. Self when the terrace on the north-side lies or the toilet a direct togang to the kitchen has, head-sake is (as we in German say): *Do it yourself!*

Your True Gisela

– 110 –

The holy mass

UNSERE DICHTER UND DENKER

Dear Peter,
it was bynear the same theatre or the same circus like
in every year. The last great book-event of this
yearhundred – yes, of this yearthousand – found as always in Frankfurt stead. But this time gave it also
some new accents on the book-mass. A whole herd of
young-german poets had just right-timy their works
on the market thrown. The critics were through the
bank beghosted, and the *Spiegel* dedicated them a
title-page. Formly can we of a sudden *Fräuleinwun-
der* in the German literature speak: Birgit Vander-
beke, Judith Hermann, Zoë Jenny, Karen Duve, Elke
Naters, Julia Franck, Jenny Erpenbeck. And these
ladies are ongively only the top of an ice-mountain. I
know not, what I therefrom hold shall. Ask me in five
years, on whom of these chicks and benjamins I me
then remember can.

So right youth-moved and topfit were this year
freely the old buttons. The greatfather-generation
was represented through the Lafontaine Oskar, the
Reich-Ranicki Marcel and the Grass Günter. These
three bedayed heroes sunned themselves before the
cameras in the light of the shine-throwers and were
not tired, always again a bath in the mass to take. Each
inch a medium-star, know they, what they the public
and themselves worth are.

The Oskar was the first, who vehement from the

– 111 –

DEUTSCHES WESEN UND DIE WELT

leather pulled. Escorted by his extreme blonded wife, marked the little gnome the big man. When the economy-world only on him hear would, would it us all better go, special the poor swallowers. But the gigantic show about Oskar's book could not hide, that the inhold rather thin is. "The heart beats left" – yes, where then else beats the heart? It smells damned after better-knowing and clever-shitting. No body out the folk will forget, that the Oskar his legs under the arm taken and himself out the dust made had, when the need and misery in Bonn on greatest was. Fullcome unfair. And now treads he with a make-work in appearance, in which he each of his earlier social-democratic comrades in the pan beats – one after the other. There goes me the hat high. More sympathetic is me there the Fischer Joschka, who fresh and free from the liver writes, how he in shortest time over forty kilos off-taken has. There can we mollies, who always an eye on the slim line keep must, only green fore envy be!

But the second greatfather, who an absolute bestseller (as we in German say) about his moved life written has, is the one and only Marcel – the literature-pope and born TV-star. His hands were shaken with devotion, and every body could not often enough hear, how deep and glowing he the Thomas Mann in his heart closed has and this year the Goethe and also, naturely, the Dostojewski and the Shakepeare. Do it again, Marcel! When he about books speaks, when he only his mouth opens, is the Book-Mass a Holy Mass. And the pope blesses the reading folk.

It comes even thicker, when we us the the third

– 112 –

UNSERE DICHTER UND DENKER

greatfather to the breast take. That the Swedish Academy this year endly our Günter outlooked and him with the Noble Price bethought has, had no pig more awaited. Late, but not too late for our Günter's ego. In Frankfurt was therefore every day a thank-god-service offholded. The price-carrier walked through all mass-halls with great solemnity and celebrated also his birthday by this occasion.

As man of the word found he for the shabby Oskar the right expressions, which us ordinary mortals not so light into the sense come would: "Hold your mouth, drink your redwine and make holidays!" And with the Marcel, who not direct a fan of the Günter is, had he without this the table-cloth between them cut – one for all times. Thereby would the Marcel with pleasures his hand out-stretch and on Günter's forgiving hope. But how long shall he still wait? He is bynear eighty.

Now must I an end find. So see we, concerned, the forehang closed and all questions open.

Your true Gisela

Gesund und schön

The inner swine-dog

ZWISCHEN FITNESS UND WELLNESS

Dear Peter,
now in spring comes it to fore-shine. When I so my tiny T-shirts out the cupboard fetch and my summerly shorts and my bikini ontry, then fall I out all clouds. Like the sausage in the peel. The mirror knows no mercy and no pity. He brings to the daylight, how I during the winter sinned have. Here a piece too much from the cream-cake, there an ice-leg, which too good tasted. Here could I not to a blackboard of chocolate no say, there had I nothing against a whole roasted chicken. Man allows himself yes apart from that nothing.

The result? Round my hip has himself an immense save-ring layed, which under the wide pullovers and coats good hidden was. But to this year's time beats the hour of truth. The poundy winter-bacon is unoverseeable. A blind man feels it with his crutch-stick, that my outer appearance not to the best changed has. When I so wider make, comes for me only still XXL in question. You can me afterfeel, that I thereover absolute not happy am. And what remains, that remains. Who has, who has. Togiven, I lost the one or other pound, when I speakwordly nothing to me took. But the normal life with all its temptations brings the weight quick again on the old tostand. It is to howling. The science says thereto: This is the yo-yo-effect – one kilo down, two kilos up.

GESUND UND SCHÖN

I tried to byplay the model-diet – the diet, which on-gively Claudia Schiffer, Kate Moss and Cindy Craw-ford always make. It goes so: One banana or one pineapple in the morning, ten litres mineral-water during the day. After two days was I ripe for the clap's mill. I saw stars the whole day over, not only in the night. This could it not be. Newly read I in the wait-room of my tooth-doctor: Six little mealtimes over the day are better than two big mealtimes. But for me are six little mealtimes much more dangerly, while I my appetite namely not in the fence hold can. Also shall man not all so eat, how it before the flint comes. Only one nice after the other, the *schnitzel* after the pommes, the onions after the tomato.

That I not laugh! In ground knows man yes every-thing – much salad and fresh vegetable. Man knows exact, what right or wrong is. This is not the problem. But the inner swine-dog comes always there-be-tween. The worst is: Man has not enough movement, man comes not from the stool high, in the bureau sits man the hinderpart formly broader and broader. There helps it nothing, when the only sport stamp-collecting is or think-sport.

What can man in such a situation do? My friend Gerda, who also good in food is, had suddenly an idea: Fitness-training! Her neighbour Klaus is newerthings halt a proud besitter of a fitness-studio. When you the training with all his machines brave befollow, guaran-tees he you really hundredpercenty, that you no prob-lems more with your body have. Klaus understands himself as promotor of the power-podex. That means: Your hinderpart will the form of a round, crunchy

– 118 –

ZWISCHEN FITNESS UND WELLNESS

apple ontake. Your skin is no longer formed like an orange. And the belly will bikini-flat be.

What for an outsight for my inner swine-dog! I was soforth fire and flame. In leggings, with calf-warmers and forehead-band – all in pink – followed I the commandos: *"And up! And up! Get fit! Get fit!"* You see, I learn also quite nice English in the fitness-studio, total byrunning. At the bar is *fatburner* and *power-food* in the offer. It goes not without pain off, and the studio stinks after sweat and deodorant. When pulse and blood-print measured were, came I me a bit like on an intensive-station fore. All in all can I freely say: Fitness makes much fun. For all see you there many people, who on the same wave-length are and who beutifull bodies have. But know you, what my Cousin Walter, this clever-shitter, newly befound? Sportlers live not longer, said he, they die only healthier. On the spot had I him on lovest the throat turned. But othersides gave he me a little to think.

Your true Gisela

Train for train

RAUCHER ALLER LÄNDER, VEREINIGT EUCH!

Dear Peter,
yes, yes, yes – you have yes so right. I should the smoking not on the light shoulder take. Blood-high-print, heart-infarct, smoker-leg, my lung bestanding only out tar and louder holes – in painting the devil on the wall are you absolute the greatest.

But how many smokers gives it, who themselves outspoken well feel in their blue mist! Think only on my two aunts, Lissy and Annie – both over eighty, and both smoke like two chimneys about the betting.

No, you can not all smokers into the self pot throw. Outerthem: Is it not richly overdriven, our little truck so on the great bell to hang? The most withburgers forget all to easy, that we smokers the state-household in order keep with our tobacco-tax. Is it then not perverse, when Father State says: Your tax is me highest welcome, but your smoking is the greatest sin on earth, which man himself think can. Us so what on to do! As if we smokers us on the self step befind like these industrialists and factory-besitters, who all their shit in masses bethinkings-loose into the blue heaven blow! Are we smokers muchlight beanswerly for the wood-dying or the ozone-hole? This is strong tobacco!

And then the newest idea from our politickers: In full earnest will they all cigarette-automates outclosely with preservers against aids bestick. What for an overrushing for a smoker! Shall he or she now mile-

– 120 –

wide for a glim-stengle run? I ask you: Must this war between not-smokers against smokers overhead be?

Direct hereto: You have no idea, how it newly on Gerda's birthday-party towent. I became my first shock in the taxi: NO SMOKING! Me fell in, that many taxi-drivers a revolver by themselves have. I know not, what harder was – not to smoke or the mouth to hold. As Gerda a passionate not-smoker is, was smoking in all her rooms absolute forbidden, basta. While she over the whole face like a honey-cake-horse grinned, must we good mine to the bad play make. And so saw this out: One group of guests was puffing on the WC, a second group in the garage and a third let the steam on Gerda's balcony off. I ask you: Is this the new life-style, on which we so long waited have? Must we us real fallen let, that we smokers like the last dirt be-handled are?

Muchlight brings a findy head one day's a cigarette with an in-built catalysator on the market, so that all tender-stringed not-smokers not more in a demon-strative cough outbreak must or a gasmask upset, when our-one only cigarette and fire out the pocket pulls. One is clear: What true tolerance is, can you from us smokers learn. Has a smoker himself ever be-heavied over a not-smoker?

Onesides: I like my cigarette – train for train. Oth-ersides: Must I smoke? No, I can every day uphear. That has already over hundred times clapped.

Your true Gisela

Nothing goes over jogging!

GRUNDZÜGE EINER WELTANSCHAUUNG

Dear Peter,
how unjust goes it on the world to! The ones eat like barn-thrashers and are slim like a bambi, the others hunger themselves through life and come not from their overflowing pounds down. Friend Gerda and I are from the latter sort – a bit roundly, unoverseebar. Gerda has a friend, and when he – fully wellwilling – to her said: I love you how you are, went she the walls high.

Newerthings bedrive Gerda and I jogging. Naive how we were, wanted we simple loose-run, just round the quarter with the bird-names-streets. After three-hundred metres did us the feets woe. That comes therefrom, said us later the friendly beserving in the sport-shop with the nice German name *Runners Point*, when man not the right shoe-work on the feets has. He could us 250 (in words: twohundredandfifty) different models of sport-shoes show. What it not all gives. There is the lay astonished, and the expert wonders himself.

But with the shoes is it longest not done. The outfit, I say you, the outfit is mindest so important, therewith you better run can. And will you from the other joggers head-shaking onlooked be, when you with your old training-suit from your volleyball-period (six years ago) upcross? Thereby gives it so dead-chic colours today. Gerda and I came total into swarming.

GRUNDZÜGE EINER WELTANSCHAUUNG

When it allerthings on the evenening to-goes and you in the darkness homewards run, is it quite, quite important, that you not under a car come. How many hares, cats and dogs have Gerda and I dead on the street lie seen – and that all only, because they not the right outfit had. Thereby thinks the sport-shop on every littleness: You can there a dress in shock-colours become, all sorts of reflectors, cat-eyes and even a complete belighting.

But this throws a light on a problem, which you not simple away-discuss can: Where can you overhead run? The streets are loud, stinking and very risky. When you freely on private ground come, can you the purest ape-theatre helive. I say you, it is not very comfortable to have the dogs behind you – or a bull, who from your shock-colour beghosted is. You can happy be, said Gerda, that they not on you shoot. What could we last week namely in the newspaper over a poor jogger read? *Father of ten children deadshot – mistaken for a rabbit!*

So see you, that also the jogging not so easy is. But everytime, when Gerda and I the jogging behind us have, our iso-drink to us take and over our grams and joules talk, feel we us roundabout happy. But then, just then comes also an appetite on a calfs-haxen up, which I with words not bescribe can …

Your true Gisela

– 123 –

Venus from Kilo

ZUVIEL SPECK AUF DEN KNOCHEN

Dear Peter,
eating holds loaf and soul together. But when you exacter underseek, what you so the whole day in your
body stuff, become you a horror. I begin with quite
little in the morning, ifwell Aunt Lissy always says: Eat
in the morning like an emperor, to midday like a king
and in the evening like a beggar. But who has already
the time in the morning, and all days is no Sunday.
The real problem is the uncontrolled eating, which
makes me fatter and fatter, when I not uppass. In this
togetherhang is eat-control exact so important like
birth-control!

And to midday? In the canteen can you only in the
fall of extreme emergency go, and when you this place
upseek, are you first right an emergency-fall thereafter. Outer, you are a friend of salted soups, soft and
juicy potatoes, fried shoe-soles and a vegetable, which
not out the tinbox is, but worse tastes. I go there from
time to time, take highest a coffee to me, and become
but the latest *klatsch & tratsch* with: That the Huber
what with his office-girl goes or that the chief highest-
personly a gigantic bump in his new Porsche driven
has. Without this ground would me no ten horses in
the canteen pull!

When you think, I had an alternative to midday,
then are you on the woodway. The "Oxen", a restaurant direct againstover, says from itself: Through-

– 124 –

ZUVIEL SPECK AUF DEN KNOCHEN

going warm kitchen with daily changing midday's table. But what they you there foreset, mocks of every description.

The fleshly ground-substance, heavy to define, is guaranteed fat and always the same. They besit freely an enormous fantasy: With champignons is it a hunter-schnitzel, with paprika a gipsy-schnitzel. With pine-apple is it Hawaii, with peaches is it California. Florida bestands out a together-scratched salad from all sorts of fruits. Tomindest are you informed, what the land-running geography so to offer has. For outlanders have they outspoken miserable photos on the card, so that no reclamation possible is: What you see is what you get.

I can eat, what I will – the bacon on the bones remains a constant factor. When I last month three kilos with unsayable pains off-hungered had, was I so proud, that I me on the way to a butcher-shop made. No, not to celebrate an orgy in flesh after this hunger-cure. I wanted only see, how heavy three kilos bacon are. A colossal mass, say I you. But what was the butcher sour, when I said: Thousand thank, now can you the bacon again awaypack. The trouble is, that I my three kilos bacon again have – knows the cuckoo how.

In the between-time have I me a little therewith off-found: I am perhaps not too thick, but ten centimetres too short. Not to forget my outspoken heavy bones, which in our family usus are. And overhead are the "mollies" again in. Some men, and not too few, like a Venus from Kilo more than a twiggy-type. Right so, I am thereby!

Your true Gisela

The po in bestform

ALLERWERTESTE PROBLEME

Dear Peter,
every day the self question, which me meterlong to
the mouth outhangs: What dress shall I onpull? Yes,
the strong sex has it there much, much lighter than
the weak sex: Trousers, jacket, shirt – ready is the
man. And we womans? We stand hours-long fore
the mirror and ask: Rock or trousers, blouse or
pullover, jacket or what? And when rock, then long
rock or mini-rock? Questions over questions and no
answers.

Have you mans to byplay the problem, that your
hinderpart so in the look-point of interest stands?
How please? Yes, thereon must we hellish eight – special when we with these supershort mini-rocks, cracky
jeans, elastic trousers or leggings carry will. Who
brings the courage up, when the figure not quite o.k.
is? By mans makes this nothing. By womans fall problems soforth in the eye.

And the po is the problem number one, there can
you gift take. Cracky shall he be and well-formed – so
sees the new fashion the po. Thereby is it not so easy,
the podex in bestform to present. Here sit halt more
and greater fat-cells than in the restly body. Chocolate, cream-cake, tiramisu – every little eat-sin is
prompt on the po off to read. And outerthem is the
skin of the po overhead not enough through-blooded.
Result: Without a regular service is the costbar hin-

– 126 –

ALLERWERTESTE PROBLEME

derpart quickly ugly and shrumply like an old apple. Had you that for possible held?

Woman makes what with. Unluckywise has my friend Gerda even more problems with the po than I. Every day pulls she a rule-right po-programme through. Under the shower takes she a special soap with extracts from mouse-thorn and hazelnut-oil. That does also the bosom, the belly and the legs good. For a better through-blooding ends she the ceremony with ice-cold water – brrrr. Thereto come all sorts of creams, lotions and gels – extra created for the all-worthiest.

But this is longest not all. Day for day makes Gerda tosetly swimming, jogging, reflex-zone-massage and a special po-gymnastic. I bewonder her, how she that all so iron through-holds. Then besits she also a massage-band with nature-brush. Equal, if dry or wet, it works like peeling (how we in German say). The nature-brush rubbles namely quite beautifull the upper horn-skin off. This is extreme important. You know self on best, what a man on no fall loves: to touch the po of a woman fuller horn-skin. Not out to think.

And what learn we thereout? Ifwell she earnest problems has, stands Gerda today not alone in the rain. She is muchmore a total happy woman, who positive thinks. Thank the cosmetic-industry is her po-skin always fresh and rosy, cracky and in bestform. Po – pardon – heart, what will you more?

Your true Gisela

Fat swims above

NIE WIEDER ODER IMMER WIEDER?

Dear Peter,
cake and chocolade, ice-cream and all sorts of sweets
– I can the fingers not therefrom let. Also when I try,
me unhomely together to take, gives it after a while no
holding more. And when first the dam broken is, can
I shore-loose what eatable in me inpush. The result is
quite naturely: 80 kilos bring I on the scales.

This heavy-weight is the endpoint, said I to me; so
can that not wider go. When you in the mirror see and
like an elephant outlook, is it with the self-eighting
out and foreby. Said, done. But how can I me overlist?
Tofirst went I into my loveling's boutique and bought
me one pair beautifull jeans – allerthings one number
smaller. And right: Tohome became I the jeans not the
legs high. But I was noway's frustrated, that was yes so
inplanned, sotosay innerhalf of my slaught-plan.

So went I then a last time pizza eating and put an orderly portion ice with cream and three beers thereon.
Then said I to me: Gisela, you must offtake! Radical
how I am, started I a null-diet. That means, there is
absolute nothing, wherewith man start can. As the
name of the diet besays: From nothing comes nothing. Only water, water, water – till I stars saw. My cir-
cle-running became bynear a collapse. My doctor lifted his show-finger and looked me seldsome on.

So went it also not. In the follow-time made I wider
some greysome experiments: Buchinger, Schroth,

– 128 –

F. X. Mayr, Atkins and who knows who still. No of this genetlemen could me help. Rice-days, apple-days, juice-days – after shortest time was alls again the same. For cakes and sweets exists simple nothing others, what me from the hocker throw could. It is to outgrow! My friend Gerda has herself outtricked, inthem she in all rooms photos of her uphanged, on which she fat and ugly outlooked. On the most pictures hung the bacon-folds only so over the girdle. I know not, I know not.

Why is in our society a beautifull woman always only a slim woman? This ideal nearer to come, make millions of girls and woman every year a diet, hunger themselves towhilen to death. I make no wits. A friend of Gerda had only one thought: How much have I eaten today, what can I me still allow? With her 164 centimetres hungered she from 68 to 41 kilos down. And now believe you it not: She thought always still, that she much too thick was. Who had her this flea into the ear set?

When the weight a life's inhold is, is it bynear too late. Then is a psychologigal damage not far away. And before it with me so wide comes, must I me lover accept, how I am. The fat politickers do this yes also. First their heavy-weight makes them so beloved in the folk.

And fat swims above, believe me.

Your true Gisela

This wool on the head!

TÄGLICHER KAMPF MIT BORSTIGEN ZOTTELN

Dear Peter,
price-question for you: what robbs me total the
nerves, what costs me a nice pole money, and what
brings me still into the grave? No, it is not my VW
beatle, ifwell he always oftener and on lovest in the
night his ghost upgives. It is also not the tostand, that
I not married am, ifwell the finance-office by us
singles quite nice tolongs – so as if by us the money
like rain from the heaven falls. It is not the politic and
these arrogant politickers, which us more and more
on palm bring, when they so wider make, us on the
arm to take.

No, I take me the right out, a fullcome personal
problem to have. My problem is my hair. Who can this
straw in form bring? I am fully fix and ready. Always
when me my best friend Gerda under the eyes comes,
packs me the pure envy. With her beautifull black-
blue locks has she so many chances by the men. How
makes she that? She, who always for a tip good is, has
by my hair the flint in the corn thrown. This wool on
the head!

And then this pig-blond colour. The grey of Aunt
Lissy is expression's strong thereagainst. What shall I
make? My hair-stylist (as we newerthings on German
say) has this and that idea. That hangs from the tofall
up. I come me middlerwhile like an experiment's
karniggle fore. What were that for times, when the

– 130 –

hair-stylist himself still *Friseur* named, later *Frisör*. Then had I not these heavy problems with my hair. Tomindest were the prices for the behandling lower.

I had the nose full and laid on me self hand on. Said, done. But my own experiments alone with the colour ended in a middler catastrophe. The result was a hair-tone between lilac and mahogany, that I ripe for the circus was. The selfmade step-cut lokked out, as if under a car come were. And the hair would and would not sit. Only one pair hours after the washing was it badder than tofore. Can you this as man overhead understand? I fear not.

What was the end from the song? I landed again by my hair-stylist. He was very tactfull, reached me a cup coffee and did so, as if nothing were: "With the right cut, special care and colour becomes man every hair in the grip!" Every hair? The result can you now on the picture see, which I you bylay. What hold you from my new hair-style?

I tell you what: Bello, the dog from Aunt Lissy, could me not more again know. He barked and barked, when I through the door incame – something, what he still never done had.

Your true Gisela

The wandering is the miller's lust

MIT GESANG DURCH DIE NATUR

Dear Peter,

we Germans are already a comic folk. Nowhere on the world gives it so many people, who the legs under the arm take and hours- and days-long over stick and stone march. As if by us cars or comfortable buses fullcome unbeknown were. Italians, French or Greeks would never on the idea come, with heavy rucksack and unformy wander-boots through Mother Nature to trample. But we come to foot. For us is no way too long and no mountain too high. In no country on the earth exists such a large and dense net of marked wander-ways.

When you – like I – a love-haver of stillness and loneliness are, is wandering the right hobby for you. Over many hours make you the experience, that no noise upcomes. You come through regions and land-strokes, where highest fox and hare themselves good night say. There can you your soul so right dangle let. But middlerwhile is stillness also not more, what it earlier was. Some wanderers have their radio with them or the handy. You hold it not in the head out!

And with the loneliness is it in some places also fore-by. Where yearhundreds long the wanderer absolute king was, cross newerthings armies of mountain-bikers the wanderer's path. No way is too stoney for these strange sport-friends, no hill too steep, no danger too great. Always must you as wanderer byside

– 132 –

MIT GESANG DURCH DIE NATUR

jump. There can you the hat high go. My tip against this plague: Grip a stick and throw it them between the spokes. Down with these rowdies on bikes!

The nicest and most important part of the wandering is the pause. You can in the grass sit and your butter-bread, egg and potato-salad under free heaven outpack. Or you stretch your bones long out, look into the blue heaven and let all you sorrows away fly. But some time-companions find the ground always too wet and cold, even in the driest summer. Never would they down-hock, it be then, they must once. In the rule wander these people so long, till they a bank find – and when they out the last hole whistle and the tongue meter-long out the mouth hangs. A king-rich for a bank!

Naturely need you a qualified *outfit* (a new-German word) for the wandering. Otherfalls are you as wanderer not for earnest taken. Under kneebound-trousers, wander-shoes, caro-shirt and a rucksack goes nothing. As professional bywork come thereto down-rolled socks, telescope-sticks and a filth-hat in question. Ifwell they not enough from the wandering become can, are the most wanderers very sharp thereon, an off-shortening of the marked wander-way to find. It is sotosay an extra sport. When they thereby not on wire are, run they headloose into their unluck. Out this ground are card and compass an unbethinged must. Or you are total on the wrong track.

What I hate, is this wandering in great groups, who loudstark through wood and field pull and one song after the other from the staple let: "Black-brown is the Hazelnut" "or "My Father was a Wandersman" or

– 133 –

GESUND UND SCHÖN

"The Wandering is the Miller's Lust". An alpenlandic variation is the art of yodeling, to byplay: "Holleri die Dudel dö". This alternative makes much fun, when you it ready bring.

But the absolute greatest joy is the direct communication with Mother Nature. The real wanderers seek halt special places up, where they an echo hear can. Therefor run they miles wide – only to cry sentences like these against the the mountain-wall: "What is the name of the burgermaster of Wesel?" The answer of the echo is naturely: "Esel". Thereover can some people themselves half-dead laugh and the trousers wet make.

You see, how wonderbar it be can, through the nature to wander.

Your true Gisela

Helps a cure-shadow?

MORGENS FANGO, ABENDS TANGO

Dear Peter,
now have I a wider field found, where we Germans the absolute world-masters are. When it halt thereabout goes, a cure to make, stand we in the first row. But what means this? Are we the healthiest or the illest folk on the world? Knows the hangman.

Every fall's was the cure by the old Greeks and Romans very in. They knew quite exact, that the healing crafts of the water better are than all pills and medicine out the chemestry. So cultivated they the bath, and for them was no better form of regeneration thinkbar.

This idea is till today fullcome the self remained – outer, that now an ill-cashbox exists, which you this extra holidays bepays. And what they today for your cure outgive, is by wide not so high, like when you tomorrow nervely and bodily total at the end are. We name this fore-sorrow. It bestands therein, that the cure an orderly programme have must, when it an effect have shall. The cure-doctor underseeks you groundly and finds out, what good for you is. A byplay: Morning's fango, evening's tango.

In a cure come many factors together, says my Cousin Walter, who it know must. He was already in Wörrishofen and in Kreuznach, in Gastein and Oberstdorf. Typical are the effects of bathing, inhalations and the climate. The climate is very important.

– 135 –

GESUND UND SCHÖN

You must only know, if you more the mountains like or more the sea. The next time will Walter muchlight to Norderney. When you as woman no children become can, gives it only one: moor-packings, day and night moor-packings. Naturely must a man also with in the play be, otherfalls helps the moor-packing overhead not. Or had you what others thought?

You see: For the cure stands a health-problem in the fore-ground. And a little bit ill is yes every body. I know freely still not, where my problems lies. Sometimes have I it in the shoulder, sometimes in the head. From time to time feel I a burn-out, as we now in Germany say. Can me a cure help?

The experts say, that the success not alone from the bathings or the mineral-water offhangs, but from a very personal moment in life: the cure-shadow. Special when the weather nice is and the sun so burns, that you it not more outhold can, then is a cure-shadow indicated. Walter means: Tomindest helps a cure-shadow, over the horrible long-while way to come, which the known-sign of every cure is. Right has he, fully right.

Your true Gisela

Ökologie für den Hausgebrauch

Let mother nature grow!

KRAUT UND RÜBEN

Dear Peter,
I say you: Eco, that is the mesh – no, not Umberto
Eco. I mean eco as it for life and nature stands. Therewith you in the picture are: I must you unbethinged
what over the garden-party tell, to which me newly
the Hubers two houses wider inloaded had. What I
from an earlier beseek in their garden beheld had,
was: All clean and orderly, all what right is. The grass
was cut two times the week, no goose-flowers or lion-
tooth in sight, all flowers in row and penis, the roses
injected with heavy gift against the louses. Short-
about: a garden, how he in the book stands, but total
dead, what eco onbelongs.

Yes my, when I now in this garden came, flipped I
out! He was not again to know. The wonderbar
straight-line barock design was total in kraut and
roots. Trees, bushes and plants were growing like in a
wild clock-forest. I was baff and asked the Huber,
what now with the louses is, which him earlier – after
his own words – over the head grew. He declared it me
hair-little: Against these beasts had he now mary-
beetles and ear-knipers. That brings it full – and no
heavy garden work more!

Only: Wherefrom had the Hubers this shining idea?
Alone come they namely not on so what. Tofirst wanted they not so right hereout with the language, then
gave they to, that they a course in the folk's highschool

– 139 –

ÖKOLOGIE FÜR DEN HAUSGEBRAUCH

beseeked had: "Ecology for the house-use" or so similar. The result: They are absolute eco-fans now. And then was she so friendly to show me their swimming-pool. They name it "wet-biotop" now, with sea-roses therein and many other plants, which I not behold can. On what they only waited: some nice little frogs and also a clapper-stork – no, not to bring the childrens, but to ingrip, when the frogs overhandtake.

The only horsefoot in this paradise on earths: Some neighbours is Huber's new-modern garden a thorn in the eye. First this shocking outlook, and then all the unkraut coming thereover into their civilized gardens. They cited Huber even before the kadi. But they became not right – the right is halt on sides of the frogs and the unkraut in this our republic! And the Huber is now always grinning: Never was it so light to lay the hands in the lap, let mother nature grow, and stand equal-timely on the top of the progress!

With green wishes

Your true Gisela

P.S. When it already a "Motherday" gives, why then not also a "Mother-Nature-Day"?

Full in the trousers

DER FLUCH DER GUTEN TAT

Dear Peter,
how man/woman it makes, is it wrong. In the last years
was us told and told, that we unbethinged what for the
around-world-protection do must. And not only the
great-industry, against the Greens always so weather,
should itself besense of a better – everyman, you and
I, should upwake and a personal bycarry thereto de-
liver.

Said, done. When we Germans of something overclothed are (equal, what it is), are we hundredpercenty thereby. The idea pulls circles, it becomes a
movement. Take the outsorting and collecting of
paper to byplay. Bynear every household in the republic puts the onfalling paper byside, staples it sorrow-foldy, makes a bind-threat thereabout and puts it
ready on the street for the collectors – or even brings
the bundle to the paper-container. I say you: Hundredpercenty.

Many people letted their liver-cheese or their fried-
sausage not only one- or twotimes inbeat from the
butcher, but three- or fourtimes. The more the better.
Those, who read one newspaper per day, bought now
two or three newspapers. It was yes so good for the
around-world-protection. Even if you came not thereto, the whole daily rubbish to read, made this nothing.
Headsake, you could your personal bycarry for a better world forewise.

ÖKOLOGIE FÜR DEN HAUSGEBRAUCH

Landup, landdown paper-containers were on evry corner upput. Whole school-classes saw the paper-collecting as a sport on. They all begripped the idea: *Recycling* (a new German word) was the device. Out old paper was new paper made – not quite so white freely, but of acceptable quality. And still what: With the money from the recycling could you a good work do. You could it to byplay to the Red Cross give or the hungry people in the third world happy make.

So wide, so good. But now fall you from the stool. Know you, what the paper-industry one good day's said? Hold, hold – we arehesticking in your mountains of paper, stop that nonsense! The price of old-paper fell so very into the cellar, so that the old-paper not more on the man to bring was. Followly said the paper-industry to the folk: Behold your paper and shit on it.

It is paradox, not true? Man does and makes, and then so what. A brilliant idea went full in the trousers. And now my problem: How shall I this the Xaverl explain, the little boy out the neighbourhood, who still so busy is, all the paper to collect?

Your true Gisela

Bird of the Year

TANTE LISSY HAT GEBURTSTAG

Dear Peter,
of my Aunt Lissy can you say, what you will. But you
can her still not to the old iron throw. Whenequal the
old dame newly with one foot in the grave stood, is she
again on the dam. When last week her birthday nearer and nearer came, was I sitting there like on hot
coals. Man goes yes not with empty hands to the cof-
fee-drinking – this says Aunt Lissy self. But what will
you a person present, who practish every thing and
every killefit has and it perhaps not more long does?
That will good overlayed be.

A poster in a show-window brought me on an idea,
when I to shopping in the town was: "Make your
friend a joy with birds!" Short and good, but which
bird? It gives yes so many sorts. And I do know my
auntie – always from finest. In the animal-shop bestood I thereupon, that it not an x-belovey flatterman
be should, but a fashionable bird. What say I – lastendly pulled I off with a chic canary-bird in a cage.

But what must I only one day later in the newspaer
read? What think you, is *Bird of the Year*? No, not my
canary, which I bought had, but the brown-little-
throat (*Braunkehlchen*). Of this bird was in the animal-shop never the speech! Such a juice-shop, me so
what on to do!

I was naturely fox-devil's wild. When I the canary
back brought, in order to exchange it against the *Bird*

– 143 –

ÖKOLOGIE FÜR DEN HAUSGEBRAUCH

of the Year, the personal in the shop looked me great on. What I me inpicture did, said they, I were well not good informed. So what must I me say let. When I inthrew, that I me on the arm taken felt, was the oven restloose out. The whole affair ended like the Hornberger Shooting.

Now come you: Would you buy a new car and no look on the *Car of the Year* throw? For what then shall it good be, that we also a *Camera of the Year* or a *Computer of the Year* have?

The customer must have a certain orientation.

One luck only, that Aunt Lissy so happy with the canary was. She has until today nothing of a *Bird of the Year* heard.

What am I evenfalls happy!

Your true Gisela

Green is the hope

EIN X FÜR EIN U

Dear Peter,
always make we us illusions. Special, when we only
the words "eco" and "bio" hear. That is a great fashion, a new trend, which us total blind makes. And
when we self us not what fore-make, are it other people, who us forth-running on the nose about-guide.
Will you byplays hear? How long believe we still, that
the "Green Point" real green is and us real wider
brings?

Rubbish is rubbish, when man nothing thereout
makes. There helps it nothing, when the rubbish a
green point has. Exact so good could it a blue moon,
a red cross or a yellow rose on the rubbish be. There
is no difference to the tostand tofore, so long namely
no pig knows, how this recycling-model landup, landdown function shall. That comes therefrom, when
man the mouth too full takes and the second step before the first does. And then read I, that some rubbish
with green points, which we so groundly outsorted
have, to India exported is or in the rubbish-burning
lands. Hold the air on!

The scandal is, that my milk-bottle, which I thousand times in the supermarket after-fill, no chance
has, a "Green Point" to become. As we a complete
trow-away-society are, becomes the predicate only,
what we away-throw. Absurd, say I. Total crazy.

And when all the points only real green were! On

– 145 –

ÖKOLOGIE FÜR DEN HAUSGEBRAUCH

the packing stands always "Green Point" to read, but on the cola-dose is the colour of the point red, on the Lila Pause is it lila, on the Philadelphia cheese is it blue. What shall man therefrom hold? As if we also no feeling more for differences had. Are we in the between-time all colour-blind? "Green" is red and lila and blue at the same time.

They make us an X for an U fore. Who three thousand "Green Points" collected has, becomes a little book gratis with the title: "Green is the hope".

Your true Gisela

It greens so green

ARCHITEKTENTROST

Dear Peter,

make we us nothing fore: On the plan look the most houses quite good out. Also as toy-model in 3D can a building a respectable figure offgive. But when the architect's product endly reality is and 1:1 in the landscape stands, rubble we our eyes, go we with the hand through the hair and murmur only: Oh my god, that can yes not true be! All the proportions are to the devil, the complete design is in the bucket, all efforts are for the cat. But so goes it sometimes, a plan is not the reality. No wonder, that the world full of ugly buildings is, often real cigar-boxes.

What do in such a situation? This is a moment, when my friend Gerda always says: Make yourself nothing thereout; the tooth of time, who already so many tears dried has, will also over this wound grass grow let. Right has she, but the shock sits first once deep. And man can yes not the whole nail-new building downpull. Who has already the chance, again from new with the planning begin? Thereby would man then exact know, what man better make can. Would man?

So or so, who helps us out such a bredouille, when a pot-ugly building there stands and so me nothing you nothing not out the world to bring is? Man must what overlay, what hand and foot has. After much after-thinking came I on this idea: Everyman is an artist, everyman can a little Christo be and his

– 147 –

ÖKOLOGIE FÜR DEN HAUSGEBRAUCH

house inpack. And in what? I say you, green is the device!

There gives it so beautifull climbing plants, which in shortest time the complete house under a green cloth disappear let. For these helprich plants has the folk's mouth already a pregnant name found, which I not in English overset can: *Architektentrost*. Special the *Knöterich*, my gardener says *polygonum aubertii*, is such a quick climber. He is instand, whole complexes of buildings in null comma nothing under masses of green total to hide. Wild wine (*parthenocissus*) and a plant with the nice name The longer the lover (*lonicera*) are also not bad. Yes, complete house-blocks and street-trains (by whose planning the architect not so good thereupon was) could on this art and wise a quite other picture offgive. It greens so green.

And all people will say: What has the architect for an original infall had! Is he not a fantastic designer, while he on every thing thinks and even Mother Nature to her right come lets? He is genial architect, a real eco-architect! And we all have not only the magnificent begreening of the house as such in our heart closed. We love also these little insects, all sorts of spiders and beatles. Not to forget the birds, which their neatly nests in the begreening build. They live with us quasi under one roof and wake us the morning's so soft out our nightly dreams. What could nicer be?

Thereto comes: Seldom can man so many flies with one clap beat. The begreening has namely also this wondersome effect: While the whole house warm in-packed is, must man not so much for the warmth-isolation do. Like from self has man it warm in the win-

– 148 –

ter and pleasant cool in the summer. So simple and naturely is the money saved, which the other people formly out the window throw, who not the chance or the luck have, in a begreened behousing to live.

And what is the greatest thing in this togetherhang? Architects, who with loaf and soul on the eco-trip are, put also a green roof on the house, sotosay as crowning of the eco-idea. They let grass on the roof grow. And this is a new sport or a fantastic eco-adventure: When you good in mountain-climbing and *abseiling* are, should it for you not too heavy be, the grass high on the roof to cut, instead before the terrace in your garden.

On all falls is it once what others for you.

Your true Gisela

Green Point and Yellow Sack

DIE FREUDEN DER MÜLLTRENNUNG

Dear Peter,

when we Germans of something overclothed are, equal what, gives it no holding more. There can we nothing for, so is our character. Here a typical byplay: When we what for the nature and the around-world do can, let we us from no other folk on earths what fore-make. There are we hundred-percenty thereby, but hallo.

But had you thought, that this folk of poets and thinkers day-daily off-falls and rubbish out-sorts? With the own hands full in the shit? Hear to: Highest personly is every time-companion landup, landdown therewith occupied, the paper, the glass, the metal and the rests for the compost piece for piece in a bevoiced order to bring. Right and order and cleanliness – your name is German!

And not to forget all the plastic, which the Green Point carries and thathalf to recycle is. The springing point, sotosay the medium, is the Yellow Sack, from which each German household hundreds besits. Before they read and write can, learn the childrens heretolands: A thing with a Green Point thereon comes into the Yellow Sack. Tofore must freely piece for piece flash-clean made be, cost it what it will. So wash I my fish-doses and yoghurt-beakers with hectolitres of hot water out. I will me yes nothing aftersay let, but makes this sense? Thereagainst stinks it devilish be-

– 150 –

DIE FREUDEN DER MÜLLTRENNUNG

fore the house of my Cousin Walter. This lazy sack holds nothing from cleanliness and throws his Green Points unwashed into the Yellow Sack. But this is for-true not the rule in this our land.

When you but think, that the whole world through the Green Point and the Yellow Sack saved be can, then have you yourself heavy in the finger cut. What must I newly out the radio hear? Many of the collected Yellow Sacks with their costbar sorted inhold wander no way's to the recycling-stations, but unbeseen into the ovens of the steelworks. Man does and makes, and then so what!

Still a wider horror-story: Is it muchlight sense-full, when hundred-thousand of Yellow Sacks with galactic sums of money to Far East shipped are? And what make they there out the plastic? Louder figures of Kim-Jong II. Without this wonder I me always more, that I sort and sort, while the costs, which I for the rubbish pay must, year for year into astronomic heights go. Must this so be? I am total sour. Can a green or yellow expert me muchlight upclear?

I would yes so thankbar be.

Your true Gisela

P.S. How brings it a great poet in these days on the point? The Green Point is the greatest swindle on earths since the colour green exists. Right has he!

It stinks to heaven

VOM REGEN IN DIE TRAUFE

Dear Peter,
the drinkwater in this our land is the best in the world.
No wonder, that Harald Schmidt of the meaning is:
Say yes to the German drinkwater! But in the high
quality lies also the hare in the pepper. I ask you: Is it
unbethinged needy, that such a water of finest standard the canalization and then the brook down goes?
Best water in colossal masses, day for day – without
every sense and understand. Out the look-angle of
ecology stand me sometimes the hairs to mountain.
Find we landup, landdown no other solutions? Can
the costbar water not better used be?

Take the toilet to byplay. Is it real the yellow from
the egg, that all the shit in every household of the
republic with the all-best drinkwater away-wash-
ed is? Can we there not better on rainwater back-
grip? Last-endly live we yes not middle in the Sahara,
but in one of the wettest zones of Mother Earth.
Rain falls by us bynear every day, sometimes still oftener.

Said, done. Germany is not only the land of poets
and thinkers, but also a nation of *tüftlers* and *bastlers*
– special in the southwest, in the *Landle*. Here catch
the people already always and eternal the rainwater
up, greatpart's halt for the bewatering of the flowers
and earth-apples in their gardens. Shortly in Leimen,
where our Great Boris way-comes, had a build-mister

– 152 –

VOM REGEN IN DIE TRAUFE

the idea, a rainwater-using-installation for the WC in his new house in to build.

A brilliant idea, but there had you the town-fathers see should. In the guess-house of Leimen was the devil loose. Rainwater in the toilet? There could yes everybody come! Today in the toilet, tomorrow in the wash-machine and over-tomorrow perhaps in the tooth-clean-glass. Very interesting were the arguments. The water, which today so from heaven falls, is shinebar also not more that, what it earlier was. The experts say, that it from heaven comes, but also to heaven stinks. Its is quasi a cocktail of poison and bacteriums. And this is the ground therefor, that rainwater self in the toilet nothing more to seek has. Horrible.

But what too much is, is too much. Some besunned town-fathers said, that it with the rain by wide not so bad be can. They gave to bethink: When the experts right have would, must yes every body, who ever his umbrella forgotten had and through the rain walked, total infected and contaminated be. Older people more then children, you Englanders more than our Italian friends. Can so what be? Who knows?

You see, the rainwater on the toilet is a problem of wide-reaching importance. No harmless business, this business with the rain.

Your true Gisela

Eat-culture?

SCHWERVERDAULICHES

Dear Peter,
"man is, what man eats". So nice can we it in German outprint. In English comes this not so good over, but I hope, you check it. When this quintessence true is, then must I say: Good night, dear friends and neighbours, the end of the mankind is only still a question of time. We eat us to death.

Every beseek in the supermarket makes us clear, when we not tomatoes on the eyes have: The apples, so beautifull they outlook, taste after styropor. Wine-grapes are the whole year over in offer, even in the coldest winter. You become a light shimmer, that some pesticides their hands with in the play have and not so light off-washed be can. The block of cheese, mantled in plastic, tastes after plastic and has the consistence of gum-bears. Yoghurt, milk and butter come guaranteed always from the other end of the republic, all the while a dairy in your neighbourhood exists, the regional milk collects and after all rules of arts into milk-procducts changes.

When you a look on the flesh out the animal-factory throw, can you with bare eyes not see, whether it anitibiotica, hormons or dioxin contains. "Life-middle" say we to all these things. But this is macabre, we should better of "death-middle" speak. What else find you in the supermarket? The rest bestands out ready-mealtimes, behandled with chemicals and thathalf

SCHWERVERDAULICHES

eatable until the year 3000. When you luck have, are some artificial vitamins bygiven. This is the end of the eat-, cook- and table-culture.

And the bread is also not more, what it once was. It begins already with the name. What heretolands earlier a "Bäckerei" was, is now a "Back-Shop" or a "Brot-Boutique". When you "Schwarzbrot" have will, are you onlooked like a visitor from an other star. But what the new names for a simple piece of bread onbelongs, knows the fantasy of the bread-designers no limits. What hold you from a "Jogging-Brot"? I look there not through. Is it special light baked, runs it from self away or is it only for joggers consumerable? Comes an "Alpenbrot" practish direct out the Eiger-Northwall, and guarantees "Sovital" a longer life? In the between-time is the sense of life total off-hand come. Shall I today the nine-corn-bread with hazelnut take or better the six-corn-bread out "controlled" biological annex or eventual the latest cry, the "Müsli-Brot"?

Overhead müsli. This find we newerthings in all thinkbar combinations: müsli-yoghurt and müsli-quark, müsli-cakes, müsli-toast and even müsli-ice. The children hold a sweet stick in the hand, which "Müsli-Riegel" called is. How man so hears, have the market-testers also müsli-hamburgers, müsli-chewgum, müsli-toothpaste and also müsli-shoe-cream in the making. But with a real müsli has all this absolute nothing to do. My Aunt Lissy says only: Bircher-Benner! This must you see, when she in the evening her self-shredded corn under water puts and in the next morning with rubbed apple, nut and what know I for

– 155 –

ÖKOLOGIE FÜR DEN HAUSGEBRAUCH

ingredients prepares. A cult-handling! Only so is it to declare, that she so stone-old is like the Queen Mum and not in dream thereon thinks, the spoon off to give.

But will I that? Will I really 100 years old be? I would already to peace be, when me a clever person this question beanswer could: What can man today overhead still eat – without that I in this moment dead to ground fall?

Your true Gisela

Liebe, Lust und Frust

The cat in the sack?

GISELA ANTWORTET
AUF EINE HEIRATSANZEIGE

Very honoured unknown man!
In this eye-look read I just your inserat, which you in
the newspaper "The World" upgiven have. Direct into
the eye falls soforth the interesting beat-line "Where
is the woman of my dreams?" While you this in English in a German newspaper formulate, hope I, that
you my English understand can. To give you a short
and pregnant answer on your question, which you
there now before all people up-thrown have: "*I* am the
woman of your dreams!"

What you true-shinely on most interest does: I can
fullfill all the from you forlonged qualifications! There
are you flat. I am still young and attractive, uncon-
ventional and have a sense for humour. That see you
on this letter already.

I am yes so happy, that you out the Kfz-branch
come. Know you perhaps, what with my old diesel
loose is? He gives in last time too often his ghost
up – namely mostliest then, when I no minute extra
over have. For you as an expert should this little fishes be.

Freely must I say, that some details of your inserat
me riddles upgive. To byplay: What means "schl., led.,
NR, r.c.?" It were better been, when you this full out-
written had. There have you the money on the wrong
end spared.

– 159 –

LIEBE, LUST UND FRUST

Naturely love I also animals. I always export the dog of my Aunt Lissy round the block. His name is Maxl, a super Bernhardiner. Whe he me so from the side onlooks, can you safe be, that he every single word from me understands. I am also romantic, special when the moon outcomes. But I am not a dark type like you, more a blond type. I hope not, that this a heavy-weighing hindernis is.

What me upfalls: You write nothing over the reading of books. That find I rather markworthy. Besit you perhaps no books, you poor man? The trend to have already a second book, is under my friends these days wide broaded. I for my person like Karl May on most. When Winnetou in the third band to die has, breaks it me every time the heart, when I this passage read.

The next point, which me a little bit perplex makes, is that you write, you have mistakes. Don't worry – as we say. Mistakes has every body, but you leave your mistakes total in the dark. Before I know, on what I me there with you inlet, be please so good, me a complete list of all your mistakes to send. Who will already the cat in the sack buy? My only mistake is perhaps, that I too fore-loud am – but not always.

I lay great worth on that, what you as next write. It is no problem for me, cultivated, feelingfull and charming to be, when it be must. That bring I locker, I swing also the dancing-leg with pleasures – the longer the lover. But I am more for tangoes and waltzes than for rock and roll.

There know you now, what with me loose is. What will you still hear? Is it important, that I in total 34

GISELA ANTWORTET AUF EINE HEIRATSANZEIGE

years on the buckle have? I for my part look more on the heart.

It does me horribly pity, that I no actual picture of me have. The photo, which I bylay, was five years ago uptaken, when my hair shorter and a little bit darker was. I also had five kilos more on the ribs then. Today is my figure more in the length stretched. Every fall's looks it so out. Short and good, I should in next time tosee, that you yourself a better picture of me make can.

Dear unknown, are you the man of *my* dreams?

With best wishes and many greetings

Your true Gisela

I silly cow

DIESE ODER JENE BEZIEHUNGSKISTE

Dear Peter,
with my friends is it a bit complicated. Many of them
have problems with their relation-boxes. Mostly runs
it so: The relation-box is still not right finished, then
is she again over the Jordan. Then must a new box
here. So goes it thereunder and thereover. Safely
comes you that Spanish fore, all Bohemian villages.
Hear to.

Gerda, to byplay, has over a half year with Christian
out the reform-house trafficked. Now has she but the
Markus, who works in a computer-shop. When he
evening's homecomes, is he innerly longest not off-
switched. Then overfalls he Gerda not with kisses and
roses, but with bits and bytes, backup and buffers.
Thereby can the Markus it all so original explain, that
even me a light upgoes: The software comes into the
hardware, by man and woman is it just others about.
But Gerda has absolute no sense for so what. And so
have I halt the befrightening, that it with their relation-box soon out and foreby is. Sad, simple sad.

Verena, with whom I from time to time swimming
go, is an outspoken beautifull man over the way run –
Jürgen. So what from good outlooking and always so
toforecoming! The only afterpart: He is still married
and has three children. That is shit, but what will man
make. Where the love tofalls, there remains she. Jürgen says, that his woman Erika the parting behinders,

DIESE ODER JENE BEZIEHUNGSKISTE

where it only plain goes. But this relation-box is even more complicated. It handles itself, when man so will, about a double-box: Wolfgang namely, Verena's ex-friend, has exact this Erika as new flame. I have freely the impression, that none real happy is. But how came it to this intermixture of the relation-boxes? As if one box alone not complicated enough were! The ground: All are in the self tennis-club, and such clubs are formly breeding-towns for so what.

Now to Hedda. She, who not in the tennis-club is, but whom I through Verena and Wolfgang know, has problems with her low frustration-tolerance. She can it not long without a partner outhold. Alone to home or in the holidays, says she, falls her the blanket on the head. And the bicycle, which she over all loves, can her also not the right bepeacing give. The end from the song: She has relation-boxes like sand on the sea. But this is not undangerous. When the Hedda newly with Jürgen on Gerda's party danced – quite hot and inny to Roy Orbison's "Only the Lonely" –, became the Verena such a flicker in her eyes: When looks kill could …

Newly said Hedda allerthings, that she for a while from men the nose full has. She must her true inner self first de-blanket and then realize. In her next holidays goes she pottering with femInIsts in the Toscana or – as she wordwordly says – to contemplations in a cloister in upper Bavaria. I am overrushed. So what were a real new train from her.

Off and to come all these friends to me, shed their heart out, weep like a castle-dog and will a good rate from me. I come me fore like a offloading-place for all

– 163 –

the littlewood from their relation-boxes. Then sit I silly cow there and shall their boxes in order bring. Who asks after my relation-boxes? I mean, the greatest mistake of these women is, that they too very love. They will them selves always with skin and hairs in the relation-box inbring, now and soforth.

And that is too much for some men – or?

Your true Gisela

When is a man a man?

DIE NEUE MÄNNERBEWEGUNG

Dear Peter,
my friend Gerda has in last time many problems –
mountains of problems, can man say. On one day is it
the figure, on the other day is it the hair-style, on the
next day is it her dress. She says to byplay: I have nothing on to pull! That is nothing new. But since one pair
weeks is she out psychological sight so very from the
roll, that I me deep sorrows make. Her dreams are so
crazy, that even friend Freud not help can. Her mother, who already three years not more unter the living
whiles, comes her night for night on the bed.

Her mother has sotosay all, but also all false made,
what man with a little girl false make can. Says Gerda.
With her soul-doctor works she the whole time up,
when she a child was. I find this not so good. When I
all upwarm would, what I as child out to hold had,
would I also not more happy be. The doctor means,
Gerda must herself from her mother loosen and her
true self find. What thinks the man, that is not so easy!
Two times went she already to pottering in the
Toscana. Gerda has there a mass people know
learned, but not her self found.

And so long she not she self is, is it naturely heavy,
with men out to come. Gerda has yes with herself
enough. There can a man make, what he will – in such
a feminine crisis stands he over short or long always in
the way. But I know by best will not, why Gerda over-

– 165 –

LIEBE, LUST UND FRUST

head so on men fixed is. I would it me thousand times overlay, before I me always the first best on the throat throw, who mostly the last dirt is.

Why claps the together-living not more so good like to the times, when greatfather the greatmother took? I think: The deeper ground is therein to seek, that the men today – like we woman – themselves a heap of problems have. Always must they what represent and themselves what foremake. You can see this trend already by the smallest boys in the children-garden. The gangy picture of a man looks halt so out: He shall strong be and cool, rich and brilliant, athletic and heavy.

When is a man a man? Already fore years confronted us Herbert Grönemeyer with this deep sorrow. After my inprint are not so very the women the head-problem, muchmore are the most men ripe for a therapy. And a new book from Sam Keen bestrongs me therein: The men are the souly cripples, not we women. Men have the civilization upbuilt, the modern society with her living standard and what not all – but they have never over themselves as men after-thought.

That must yes once said be, bravo! The strong sex is in reality horribly soft and weepily. But we women are yes not so. Perhaps can we thereby behelply be, the strong sex again up to right. But here says Sam Keen: Think you – not with you women. He is therefor, that the man bye-bye to the woman says. The man comes out the woman, and the woman is him his whole life thereby hinderly, to him self as the true man to find. There must I me but very wonder. Are the men always

– 166 –

DIE NEUE MÄNNERBEWEGUNG

the beshittened and the gelackmeiered? There is the dog in the pan crazy. This puts the whole world-history from head to the feet.

What this story with Gerda to do has? See you, here closes itself the circle: Can we – women and men together – not a way seek, our individual self to find? Women *and* men?

Your true Gisela

I mean it only good

SCHEIDUNG VORPROGRAMMIERT?

Dear Miss Sophie,
bald will you the Edward, the youngest son of Queen
Elizabeth, as man take. I wish you thereto much luck.
And luck is it, what you bitterly needy have will. Do,
what you not let can, it are my beans yes not. But I can
me not help: In your fall have I stark the feeling, that
you not quite in the picture are, what there on you to-
comes.

Or shall it you one good day's so go like the other on-
married princesses? Look only, what with the Diana
and the Fergie happened. In the beginning were they
named *The Lusty Wives of Windsor*. But in reality had
they it not so light, they must every spleen of their
men out-bathe. After years of horror and many
newroses had they expensive therefor to pay, that
their royal princes total corksed are. How blind must
man be, when man this not more clear sees: With the
Windsor boys is not good cherries eat. They are outspoken slack tails and overthis lame bottoms, how
they in the book stand. Out the sight of a woman can
you them in the pipe smoke. When they as a man
asked are and you as woman to side stand should, give
they little by and make themselves out the dust. Is this
a rosy future?

The Charles to byplay stands fullcome under the
royal slippers of his mother and father. When they a
might-word speak, pulls he the tail in and whimpers

– 168 –

SCHEIDUNG VORPROGRAMMIERT?

like a little poodle. He says to all yes and amen. In such situations stood the poor Diana mother-soul's alone on wide floor. She was total over-demanded. And this was without doubt the ground therefor, that she it in the palace no longer outhold could and direct into the arms of the next best riding-master ran. When I you so on a photo in the "Neue Post" see, falls me up, that you the Diana exact out the face cut are. If this a good sign is?

The turn- and angling-point in the whole kings-house is naturely the Queen. In the moment thinks she freely only of her golden jubilee in the year 2002. Then will she with all pomp celebrate, that she before fifty years the thrown climbed has. And the Charles, who the whole time on King learned has, will widerto no chance become. There can you see: The Elizabeth has no heart for her children, highest for her royal dogs and horses. When you you with her good-stand will, must you your half life with her on the backs of horses tobring. Will you that?

The Queen Mum is a phenomenon, she is overhead not little to become. The more she on the hundred to-goes, the friendlier is her personality. When you with her from time to time a little whisky drink, is she already very to peace with you. And she will naturely a good word for you by the Queen inlay. Quite others sees it with the Prince Philip out. I warn you, he is so something like a royal scratch-brush and very high-nosy. When you from the Philip some off-stand hold, will it you not bad go.

Why you the Edward into your heart closed have, must you self on best know. He has openbar some out-

– 169 –

standing qualities, which till today not so right to fore-shine come are. He is more or less an unbewritten leaf. But who knows, what he with the boys and girls from the theatre so all employed has. Out my sight are these artists louder hallodries. I in your place would the Edward groundly on heart and kidneys overproof, before I him the yes-word give.

And then must you with all calculate. On every fall need you a good right-bystand, therewith you after a separation not with empty hands there stand. The Diana to byplay had an excellent advocate. He could say and write 17,5 million pounds for her from the Charles outknock, when they separated. The Fergie thereagainst had not so much luck with her separa-tion. She was with less than half a million pounds off-found. So comes it, that the Fergie bynear on the hunger-cloth nibbles. Poor girl.

Dear Sophie, I mean it only good. I will the best for you. Overlay it you still once, before you into your un-luck run. A sea of tears is always the end.

Your true Gisela

Can that good-go?

STEFFI UND DIE LIEBE

Dear Peter,

how you know, had we Germans terrific much luck,
what the tennis onbelongs. Before 1985 were we so
good like an underdeveloped land in this sport-art.
And then came our Bobele, the Becker Boris, to Wim-
bledon and showed all world, how man real tennis
plays. A short while later was also the Graf Steffi famous as global tennis-queen.

No wonder, that our folk total beghosted from these
blood-young heroes was. The both and the Weiz-
säcker Richard were world-wide the personified symbols of a better Germany. When you now by us in
every cow-village a tennis-club find, goes this on the
unhomely enthusiasm toback, which itself thank Boris
and Steffi landup, landdown like a running fire out-
broaded has. Even in our eastly fatherland exist blossoming tennis-landscapes. In the beginning of their
careers thought man yes for a while, that these two
young creatures their shoes together under one bed
put and the national dream-pair per excellence offgive would. But cough-cake, the love can – as every
child knows – not calculated be, not on devil come
out.

The Boris and the Steffi made their way with different partners and different trailers – he for milk and
she for noodles. But always looked the Steffi a bit too
earnest and very lonely out, also when one triumph

– 171 –

LIEBE, LUST UND FRUST

the other hunted. Fact is: Over ten years were the two tennis-heroes in superform. When the tortured and tired bones not more so with-played, came the great shock. First the Boris, then the Steffi hanged their sport from one day to the other on the nail. The whole nation stood before the heavy question: Gives it a life after Boris and Steffi?

Not to forget: also our Schumi Michael is away from the window. The real heroes die formly out. In this stadium of deepest national depression passed a wonder. The Steffi and the Agassi! They cuddled and kissed in all publicity. All came very, very overrushing and quick. Seven years had the Steffi a friend, what you yes not so light off-shake can like a wet dog the water. And then so what – straight just the Agassi, this tennis-clown! What for an adventurely outfit had he in the last years not all to best given: colourfull cyclist-trousers, meter-long hair, an ear-ring, pirate-look with a head-cloth, lacquered finger-nails and razored legs. And the Steffi? Brave and unshinebar to the goes-not-more. But now is she openbar in the seventh sky.

Naturely is the whole German folk moved and touched – after all, what the poor Steffi so with- and through-made has, special with her father. My Aunt Lissy come the tears into the eyes. Endly is the Steffi openbar righty in love, roundabout happy. So easy and relaxed have we her still never in her life seen. But in this moment of highest happiness fall also some drops of vermuth into the sweet wine. Is the Agassi the right man for's life? In this point have we yes so our be-thinkings. Can the paradise-bird from Las Vegas our Steffi in his 24-rooms-villa real happy make?

STEFFI UND DIE LIEBE

One effect of this love-affair springs freely quite clear into the eye: The Agassi has a phantastic come-back (as we in German say). After he so tennis-tired was, that he on place 141 in the world-rank-list down-slipped, is he now the absolute number one, since he the Steffi in his arms closed has.

There can you see, what the love in the tennis-sport bework can. It is an art of doping – the only doping, which not forbidden is. In this sense wider thought: It lies formly on the hand, who the absolute Wimbledon-Champions in the year 2020 be will …

Your true Gisela

Aus der Traumfabrik

So what comes from so what

„EINE VERHÄNGNISVOLLE AFFÄRE"

Dear Peter,
newly made my friend Gerda the fore-beat, in a film
to go. Not just a film – but the film, about whom all
world speaks und who ongively hair-exact the time-
ghost meets: "Fatal Attraction" is the title. By us in
Germany have they this thereout made: "Eine verhängnisvolle Affäre".

From what the film handles? There is the Michael
Douglas to see, his mister father Kirk Douglas direct
out the face cut. He plays a fash yuppie, who the
bound for's life with a nice little wife closed has. He
names also a sweet thing of a child his own, a rabbit
and a fine little house. All could outspoken paletti be.
But one good day's runs a great, long-leggy, unhomely sharp blondie the Michael over the way. He can not
"no" say. Soon sit they by dish and candle-light and
throw themselves much-saying looks to. Naturely
knows every cinema-goer, who a bit on wire is, how
this ends – in bed. And so comes it also. Lusty, how
the Michael not quick enough out his trousers step
can. Hot is the air, and the man and the woman bego
marriage-break after streak and thread.

So wide, so good. Now come such escapades already
in the bible and today in the best families fore. But
with this blondie has the Michael himself heavy in the
finger cut. She can namely the throat not full enough
from him become. He othersides will out this overhot

– 177 –

AUS DER TRAUMFABRIK

affair outstep, but the sharp blondie lets him absolute
not in rest. She foreseeks selfmurder, ruins his car,
puts the lovely rabbit of Michael's family in the soup-
pot and goes with a long butcher-knife on Michael's
wife loose. In last minute comes the Michael there between. He can the blondie in his bath-tub under water
press, and Michael's wife gives her the rest with a
shoot-iron.

So what have you not seen: To this bloody finale
clapped the to-lookers in the cinema loud byfall out
full soul! Gerda and I were total out the socket – not
over the film, but over our time-companions.

This film will us on devil come out whitemake:
From an unforsighty side-jump become you eventual
not aids. The result of such an adventure is muchmore, that always a behammered and blood-thirsty
lovehaver on your mat stands and you the hell hot
makes. So what comes from so what. This is a warning. The family is in danger, if not the whole evening-
land. High live the true house-little-mother! Thathalf:
Kill this blondie, this rat, this devil!

No, thank you – not with us, my dear. That goes full
against us womens – always good for coffee-cooking
and bed-making, so long the lord and master his joke
thereby has. With full-steam back into the fifties, if
not into the nineteenth yearhundred! I say you, that
make we upcleared womens and girls not with, that
has our-one absolute not needy. Such time-ghost can
me stolen be!

Your true Gisela

– 178 –

... *that the walls only so wobble*

ERST KRIEGEN, DANN BEKRIEGEN SIE SICH

Dear Peter,
no, when all world in the cinema streams, can I not
backstand. Overall gives it now only one great theme:
"The War of the Roses". There have you no chance:
When you not in the film were, can you overhead not
withtalk. You look very old out, when you so opensightly behind the moon are.

But what is it about sky's will, what this film so attractive makes? What comes there over? A total riddle for me. Why are the people so beghosted, when
Michael Douglas and Kathleen Turner themselves
from life to death promote? But, sorry, this is already
the great finale, when they both from their misterly
crown-lighter in the depth fall.

Too, too nice, how the film begins. My friend Gerda
said, so right was for's heart. Michael and Kathleen
learn themselves know and love, have two lovely (a little too fat) childrens, a dog, a cat and a wonderfull
house. And when they not died are, then live they still
today. While I am not from yesterday, knew I soforth,
that so what not long good go can.

And right, what say I, this typical American Dream
explodes like a soap-bladder. That came so: When
Michael one day's ill is and thinks, that his last hour
beaten has, will she nothing more from him know. She
makes him clear, that he himself to the devil scissors
shall. My God, and that so short before the silver wed-

– 179 –

ding. There had she these pair years still wait could. She sets him behearted the stool fore the door and will only the house behold. But herewith has she the right nerve by him met: The house is also his one and all.

So what from outspoken fetischism have I long not more seen: Town that they sell the house, part the money through two, go their ways and let the dear god a good man be, befight they themselves from now, that the walls only so wobble. Every middle is them right, also under the girdle-line. And they let themselves what infall: He pinkles to byplay over the fish, while she guests has. But she stands him in nothing after and makes postturning his beloved oldtimer flat like a pancake. Horrible and unappetitely, say I only. I have one please: He-spare me more details. On lovest were I out the cinema gone, but then had I not the seeing's worth finale with the crown-ligter withbecome. To last is the beautifull house only littlewood. Clap closed, ape dead.

And the moral from the story? Dear people, behandle your partner a little bit lovefuller. And take yourselves together. Then when you a knife between the ribs have or with your partner from the crown-lighter fall, goes you too late a light up!

Your true Gisela

And when they not dead are ...

EINFACH HERZZERREISSEND

Dear Peter,

this film runs and runs heretolands, and endly know I
also, from what the people so swarm: "Pretty
Woman". What shall I say? The love gives us always
riddles up – special in America, where dreams so nice
are, that they unbethinged true be must. But let me
beautifull the row after tell.

First comes there Richard Gere in the picture, the
ultimate dream-man, worldwide the swarm of all
womans' hearts from nine to ninety. He plays a rich
yuppie, who but poor in his feelings is. How says the
poet: Money can't buy him love. Richard overtakes
bankrott firms for one million dollars, sells them for
three millions, and from the three percent win lives
he – not bad.

But one nice day's crosses Julia Roberts his ways –
the pretty woman. For all cinema-goers, who no look
for so what have or blind are, sings Roy Orbison the
song "Pretty Woman". The only hook is, that Julia as
lust-object on the Hollywood Boulevard works – the
Reeperbahn of Los Angeles. Richard forks her there
up and rents her for a week, like he a car rent would.
But in his fine circles falls the Julia total up. As uncomplicated girl from the street is she the ground for
many complications. And so brings he the Julia by,
how man with the right credit-cards the right dress
becomes. She learns also quick, the salad with the cor-

– 181 –

rect fork to eat and how man to Verdi's "La Traviata" the tears a free running lets.

But knows the hangman why – so right will the love-story not in the gangs come. In the costbar midnight-blue silk-bed of the two is nothing loose, absolute dead trousers. But how they so afterthink, find they out, what by both the same is: "We both lay people on the cross for money."

Wonder, oh wonder – after a while is the ban broken, and they come there-behind, what true love is. How would Grace Kelly and Bing Crosby sing: Love for ever true. But before the film to end goes, must Robert and Julia still a thirst-stretch behind them bring. It shines, as if all out and foreby were. But this happens only out dramatic grounds. In the great finale namely fetches the prince his ash-puttle out the tower. He befrees her from her miserable life on the street between the junkies, dealers and toholders. Too, too nice!

And when they not dead are, then live they still today. Naturely had I tears in the eyes. I fetched my hand-cloth out the pocket. Absolute first class, what man so together-dream can.

Your true Gisela

Weeping like a castle-dog

DIE URGEWALT DER „TITANIC"

Dear Peter,

I must you unbethinged what from a mega-event tell: Again is the Titanic undergone – this time in the flood of Oscars, in a sea of human tears and in the masses of money, which the film in-plays. World-wide is the bear loose. All folks of this earth will the gigantic show-play on devil come out see. You believe it not. They run in hordes into the light-play-houses and stand snake, as if it there what for gratis gives. And all world riddles: What is it, what this stripe has and what other stripes opensightly not have?

Now must I inroom, that I fore louder stress no time found have, this film of all films to see. Thereby lies my cinema quite in the near. But the longer I thereover after-think, say I to me: Is it real a catastrophe? Must I me the make-work onlook? Goes me what off in life without the Titanic? The winner is: Three times "no".

I miss nothing, in contra-part. The life around me is complete filled with the Titanic – day for day. Newspapers and TV bring always again pictures and brew-warm stories. If I will or not (mostly will I not), tell me all people what out the film. The love-story and the undergang goes them so deep to the heart, that the pump only so over-flows. How says the poet: Of what the heart full is, of that goes the mouth over.

Middlerwhile know I so many details of Rose and Jack, of the upper decks and the lower decks, that I

– 183 –

AUS DER TRAUMFABRIK

me ask: Have I the melodrama self seen or have I not?
The others come overhead not on the idea, that I one
of the rare persons am, who in reality no shimmer has.
And what is it, what all hearts higher beat lets? Emo-
tions, sensations, dramatic effects, great cinema –
endly a film, which the best of "Doctor Schiwago",
"Rhinegold", "Shining" and "2001: Odyssey in the
world-room" together-brings. I personly would yes
lover Tom Cruise and Nicole Kidman as "Romeo amd
Juliet in the water" see. But so wide are we still not,
that every body his own film make can.

The Titanic is like a drug. My friends flip total out,
women and children to first. Helga has the three-
hours-opus already three times seen, Maria was five
times in the cinema. Even my friend Jan, generally
known as an outspoken room-hocker, holds it no
longer in the house. And every beseeker is weeping
like a castle-dog. Hours after the show-play are the
eyes so red like those of angora-rabbits. An end of the
catastrophe is overhead not in sight.

Know you, what I think? The luxury-liner Titanic
lies in first line not deep in the Atlantic, but as myth-
ical *klops* middle in the soul of us all. And how real is
the reality? Only as picture can we the world still understand.

Your true Gisela

Holy straw-sack!

WIE ES DER ZUFALL SO WILL

Dear Peter,
since some weeks is here only one theme in all mouths. It was not the sun-darkness, which I without damage on body and soul happy overstood have. In these days lie me all people heavy in the ears. They say: You must unbethinged into this film "Notting Hill" go, the greatest summer-hit of all times. When also my friend and neighbour Jan together with his better half Maria formly on me inworked, gave it no holding more.

My bosom-friend Helga was also with from the party. With a bucket full popcorn and one litre cola begave we us in the cinema and waited on the things, which there come should. To first treads Hugh Grant in appearance, and prompt is it all womans from eight to eighty so warm around the heart. But here can us the smart Hugh only sorry do. As bookhandler for travel-books has he also already better days seen. His wife has him the running-pass given. Therewith he not mother-soul's alone is, lives he with this Spike together. But the type is total from the roll. I ask me freely, how man this crazy madman outhold can, who the whole house to a madhouse made has.

Then comes the Julia Roberts into the picture. She plays herself, namely the mostest famous filmstar of the world. As such has she the idea, through Notting Hill to walk. Simple so. Is it then the possibility –

– 185 –

AUS DER TRAUMFABRIK

without bodyguard and without police? Wonders gives it always again. The diva steps down from heaven and begives herself under us shabby people. She boots into Hugh's down-come shop and will a book about the Turkey have. Why only must it the Turkey be? Why not a book about Greece, Italy or the Philippines? We know it not, and it plays also no violin. The Julia leaves the shop, and the Hugh throws her his beknown dachshund-eyes-look after. Out and foreby!

But how it the tofall so will, meet the two after some minutes again on the street together. And as tolpatsch, how he in the book stands, sheds the Hugh the Julia a beaker orange-juice over her T-shirt. What shall I say, a beaker? She looks out, as if it a whole canister been were. But the Hugh is full the cavalier, takes her to home and lets her there the wet T-shirt change. Before she goes, presses she him a little kiss on his mouth. Hey, that was it? No pig understands, what there off-goes. A total riddle.

The film is full of hick-hack, very late land the Julia and the Hugh in bed. And what there to see is, can you children not only from, but also *under* six years show. I had stark the feeling, that the Hugh his undertrousers in bed onbeholded had. With the Julia Roberts in bed and then the under-trousers on! Holy strawsack. One night are the two in a little park. What could I me only in my fantasy out-paint! But in reality happens nothing. What binds these two characters, who from so different worlds stem, together? We know it not. The absolute star in this scene is this beautifull English park-bank out wood, from where the camera into the heaven glides.

– 186 –

WIE ES DER ZUFALL SO WILL

And then the old trick: Finds the love-pair lastendly together? Yes or no? The Julia goes, the Julia comes. Through tofall makes she again a film in London. Somehow comes me the happy end like a tragedy fore: The little bookhandler is now a prince – a manly bywork on the side of the famous diva. And when they not dead are, so live they still today. The park-bank has longest not out-served in the film. The Hugh sits there, and the Julia lies there – the pretty woman with an enormous pillow under the dress, where she under normal circumstances a total slim belly has. We shall think: A child is under way's – but howso, from the Holy Ghost?

What me also very, very wondered has: Every body in Notting Hill speaks flowing German. And it is a good German, which out the mouth of the show-players comes. Yes, when that so is. The next time, when I on the Portobello Market shopping go, will I my English better to house let and there only my mother-speech to best give.

Your true Gisela

Es weihnachtet sehr

Christmas-tree on the backtrain?

DIE LEHREN DER WEIHNACHTSÖKOLOGIE

Dear Peter,
to buy or not to buy, that is here the question. Shall I
me this year a christmas-tree besorrow or shall I not?
I am total unsafe. Some people say: We are solikeso
enough confronted with tree-dying, why shall we
formly trees murder? Is it needy, that we Germans as
a folk of tree-murderers onseen are – and that outcal-
culated to the high-holy christmas-feast?

Thereagainst mean wide befolkning's circles, that
man a christmas-tree without bethinking buy can. The
ongively persil-shine: The christmas-trees of today
grow only in plantages. And in the plantages is absolute no nature more ontomeet. Out ecological sight
is there alls dead, mouse-dead. Alls is quasi green on-
stricken. And deader than dead goes now really not.

Exact out this ground now is the christmas-tree for
other people, who still others think, a thorn in the eye.
What these time-companions say, makes me weak: On
the fields of the platages could plants grow, which
much worth-fuller are than these christmas-trees. To
byplay flowers, which in outdying begripped are. As
this not the fall is, comes it to the following consequence: While the unbeteachable folk of Germans
year for year every season on the christmas-tree in
every household bestands, are more and more land-
strokes like wild upforested. So comes it, that blos-
somig landscapes to total dead plantages made are.

– 191 –

ES WEIHNACHTET SEHR

Some of my greener friends throw allthethings here in: When you already against a christmas-tree are, then must you a correcter begrounding for your boycott have. And the only stich-holdy ground is in their eyes the fact, that the real and only true-German christmas-tree himself on the backtrain and thathalf on the Red List befinds. Had you so what thought? The christmas-tree must heretolands protected be and may highest out the outland come. But how can I poor wife on the market know, if I a real inland's tree, an aftermade sort or import-ware before me have? Equal expensive and very expensive are they all through the bank.

That call I problems, my dear mister singing-club! The alternative would yes a plastic-tree be, which you every year cultural recycle can. Or you have a personal tree in the forest, which you year for year on the Holy Evening beseek, like a dear old friend on the church-yard. How also always: On every fall had you the forepart, that then the needles not downfall, when you only begin,with the christmas-songs to sing.

In this sense wish I you a happy Christmas, my lover, and a beautifull bescissoring!

Your true Gisela

– 192 –

Sweeter the bells never cling

VOLL IM WEIHNACHTSSTRESS

Dear Peter,
from outside, from wood come I here, I must you say:
It christmasses very. How wonderbar is it heretolands
now in our world fuller angels, moons and stars, apples, bells and hearts. All these christly symbols can you
in red, gold and silver have, with glitter and glimmer,
in big and in little. The first domino-stones and life-
cakes were in the supermarkets in September seen.

Sweeter the bells never cling in the shops and buy-
houses, in the streets and on the christchilderl-mar-
kets. By the stand, where I me off and to a pizza inpull,
doodle they normalerwise "O sole mio". But now can
you from mornings to evenings "Still night, holy night"
hear. The sharpest decoration: pizza with lametta.

Christmas stands before the door, but before it so
wide is, rotate I still through. With other words: I am
full in christmas-stress. And every year the self circus,
which me meterlong to the throat hangs. What for a
christmas-tree this time? Alone this question brings
me on the palm. One from the tree-school or one out
plastic? A white tree with red candles or a red with
lilac bullets? Dead-chic, means Gerda, but then pass
not the selfmade straw-stars from last year thereto.
Problems over problems.

And every man awaits what from me – my aunts and
my sister, my friends and, and, and. When I only one
forget, is the devil loose to christmas. Aunt Lissy to

– 193 –

ES WEIHNACHTET SEHR

byplay is longest not to peace with one pair nice pocket-cloths and the Regensburger dome-sparrows on CD. No, I self must her also what to the guitar sing, while it her so on the heart goes. Shall I her what whistle this year? No, you can not so greysome be to the high-holy feast, not then. We shall overcome, as the poet says, but for's first come I not to me self. No chance more by the outbooked hair-stylist (as we in German say), I look out like a horror-screw.

Oh stress let after! Cousin Walter, who no child of sadness is, has himself right-timely to Gran Canaria offset. But christmas on the strand in bikini? No I stand more on a little bit snow and silence. I think I go in me and bring the time over christmas in a cloister to – when they only there TV have. Over christmas come namely always so beautifull films.

I wish you happy festivities and many presents from the christ-child, sorry, you Englanders have yes the Father Christmas.

Your true Gisela

From heaven high

DIVERSE WÜNSCHE ZUM FEST

Dear Peter,
man learns nothing thereto. There think you months-
long thereover after, it next time quite others and better to make, but then is all again the same – every year
the same stress to Christmas. Already in the fore-field
of this high-holy feast can you the hat high go!

So is it extreme heavy, a present for a person to find,
who already all has – even the water-kettle from
Alessi, the original railway-station-clock from Marl-
boro or an ugly lamp name's Tizio. There falls me
nothing more in – end from the song. It be then, you
come on the idea, what to present, which so outfallen
and crazy is, that so light nobody thereupon comes.
How were it to byplay with an overrushing good tast-
ing *Edelzwicker* from Aldi, with a chic and warm
pullover from C&A or with a real nice stool from
Ikea?

Overhead is Christmas not more that, what it earlier was. Last year wondered I me already, that Aunt
Lissy electric candles from the christ-child have
would. But his time understand I the world not more.
Since Aunt Lissy halt bungee-jumping in television
seen has, is she fullcome beghosted and absolute hot
thereupon. Muchlight, so says she, is it good for her
rheumatism. She wishes herself really a good-shine
for a jump. Aunt Lissy from heaven high – sotosay as
christmas-angel. If she that overlives?

– 195 –

ES WEIHNACHTET SEHR

Maxl, the youngest son from my sister, is total out the little house. No wonder by this reclame, from which nobody loose comes. His wish-list is every day longer and longer. In his dreams carries He-man fights out with devils and dinosaurs, with Alf and Captain Bluebar. But the figure, with whom Maxl on lovest plays, is "Guy the Gorilla" – in my eyes a horrible ape-monster.

Thereto know I a nice little history from last year. It begave itself to the time, when my sister and Maxl to Holy Evening the christmas-tree decorated. They were nearto ready, only the great christmas-angel, a traditional family-piece, was still not outpacked. My sister asked a bit secretfull: "And, what think you Maxl, comes on top of the christmas-tree, something special and very beautifull, sotosay the absolute crowning?" Maxl 's prompt answer, it was no question for him: "Guy the Gorilla".

Since this thinkworthy day has now the christmas-angel his own name in the family – *Guy the Gorilla*, from heaven high!

In this sense wish I you a many, many nice presents!

Your true Gisela

Joseph & Jesus

NEUE BERUFLICHE ALTERNATIVEN

Dear Peter,
not all, what in the bible stands, can you for bare coin
take. This is yes since longer beknown. Experts go
even one step wider and say: The bible is more a book
of phantasy than a product of reality. But the newest
news from the front of the bible-researchers puts our
religious world-picture very in question – special,
when it about our christly feelings to this time of the
year goes.

The speech is of the greatest event of the evening-
land, all years again: Christmas in the stall of Bethlehem. Ox and donkey spend natural warmth. Also the
restly materials are ecologically valuefull – the crib,
the stall out wood, the roof, the energy-saving belighting from heaven. And no ugly pampers for the
holy child; there lies it, ah children, on hay and on
straw. How have we this special *Gemütlichkeit* since
our children-days loved!

This wonder-nice scene had only one big, big mistake. Offseen from the ecological background, lets
the message very to wish over. The situation in the
stall of Bethlehem is so what from poor and poorly,
that it knows God no fore-picture for our perform-
ance-society be can – no incentive for dynamic
managers, no kick for our younger generation, who
for a place in the sun fights. And there is absolute
no *Ruck* in sight, which loud our Federal Presi-

ES WEIHNACHTET SEHR

dent through our land go shall, highest Joseph's rucksack.

Bynear 2000 years was this so, till the Holy Ghost a certain Professor Giovanni Magnani in Rome homeseeked and him the following inspiration ingave. Jesus had in reality no poor parents, they were muchmore stink-rich. This is everyfall's the quintessence of the professor's book under the nice title "Jesus, Builder and Master". The sensation is perfect.

But what are now the consequences of the ghost's flash of Professor Magnani? First: We must groundly up-room with the ideology of religious poorness, which we so long cultivated have. Endly goes a *Ruck* from the bible out, an economic impulse for our down-hanging society. Second: We must correct our picture from the good old Joseph out the bible. He was halt not the simple tabler, perhaps a weak-head, as whom we him since 2000 years seen have. In reality was Joseph a clever built-engineer, true-shinely a busy undertaker and shop's man. And Jesus was an architect, with safety a member of the middle-stand and not a poor swollower. It is throughout possible, that Joseph and Jesus as partners together-worked and a cooperative workshop with a bureau in Nazareth had: *Joseph & Jesus*.

Now is all clear, so after and after falls it like sheds from the eyes. Only an architectonic profi could to by-play a sentence like this formulate: You are Petrus the Rock, and on this rock will I my church build.

Your true Gisela

All years again

WEIHNACHTEN IM INTERNET

Dear Peter,
to this time of the year play all people crazy. They have a screw loose. Where you also stand and where you also go: You are overall over-showered from Christmas – on the streets and on markets, in the shops and in the churches, in the houses and in all television-channels. The heavenly army-troops sing it loud from far and near: "Sweeter the bells never cling", "Tomorrow comes the Christmas-Man", "Daughter Zion, joy yourself". But the absolute tophit is "Still Night". Harry Belafonte sings it and Bing Crosby, Karel Gott and Julio Iglesias, Heino, Cindy und Bert, not to forget Bill Clinton, who it on the sexophone plays. And I? I am dreaming of a White Christmas.

Alone, when I of the Christmas-Tree think, could I me terrible uprain. Why must it overhead a fir-tree be? In this togetherhang are we people of the warm-temperate zones quite nice in forepart. What kind of a tree do the people for Christmas take, who in the desert live? A cactus or a palm-tree? How looks this then out! A cactus or a palm-tree decorated with candles, colourful bullets and lametta is so like a Pentecost-Ox on a snowboard. Oh fir-tree, your dress will me what teach. In this year are the trees full of gift, while the plantation-besitters too much pesticides on the Christmas-Trees injected have. From heaven high.

ES WEIHNACHTET SEHR

And then the Christmas-Markets, which always earlier start, newerthings already middle November. Life-cakes, domino-stones and pepper-nuts become you already in August. Fresher goes it not. As if all bakeries for Heinrich Böll's aunt bake would, who round about the whole year Christmas has. Overall see you things, which you in your whole life not need, but which you ongively in the right mood for Christmas bring. To the unsayly outfit of these markets belong rustical wood-huts, glow-wine-stands, the selling of bonsai-trees, kitschy marzipan-figures and bird-vote-whistles. People, who under normal condition total sober and serious are, carry now Nicholas-Caps on their heads with blinking light-bommels. They eat fatty rub-cakes and absorb buckets full of glow-wine, a sticky stuff, which they there-home never touch would. But here on the market drink you for a good purpose, special at the stand of the Rotary Club. With pleasure take you there one or two glasses more. Come, you shepherds.

On the third Advent-Sunday, was the hell loose in the city. Tenthousands of beseekers tortured themsleves through the footgangster-zone. Hereby, oh you creditors. A whole folk in consumption-ecstasy, from all good ghosts left. And all in a horrible stress. Who can there still quiet blood beware? It gives no escape, no chance for a backtrain. Under this burden break I together. I can not more. And every year the same procedure as last year: There went an order out from the Emperor Mammon, that on earths profit to make is, cost it what it will. As if it so in the Bible stands. All years again.

– 200 –

WEIHNACHTEN IM INTERNET

Will it under such circumstances not better be, this whole circus up to give? I have there an idea. We should Christmas from now on in the internet bego. The internet is namely the new universal-religion. Without stress sit you there-home, surf through the Christmas-Forest, visit Snow-White and the Seven Dwarfs, how they the high-holy feast bego, and finish all your shopping in a virtual Harrods or Disney World Christmas-Market. The *real* environment will us from whole heart thankbar be – no stop and go on the autobahn, no benzin-consumption, thathalf no stinky air. Is this not fantastic?

In the time B.B.G. (before Bill Gates) lived the Christmas-Man real in Himmelpforten and besat a branch-site in Himmelsthür. Now is all others. Under the address *www.himmelpforten.de* has also he his gates (!) in the internet opened. The good man will your children gladly an e-mail send. I am flat, he is firm in German, English and Svenska.

Dear Peter, I wish you what – sleep in heavenly rest.

Your true Gisela

Bang-bang

ALLES GUTE FÜR Y2K!

Dear Peter,

now, there we the high-holy feast just overstood have and so happy are, that the christmas-goose not more heavy in the stomach lies, stands the next stress before the door. The speech is of the year 2000 or the millennium, as some cultivated people say. On this magic cipher stares all world like the bunny on the snail.

Thereby exists this year 2000 in reality overhead not, it is only a fantasy in our heads. To byplay was Jesus already four years before our time-counting born. When this not irritating is: Jesus was born in the year 4 before Christ's birth! This would mean that the Millennium longest passé is, namely since the year 1996. And what was 1996 loose? Nothing spectactular. Prince Charles parted himself from the Di, the Schröder Gerhard from his Hillu, and the Telekom went to the purse. Poor millennium.

But self, when we this fact ignore, will the turn of the yearthousand only from the 31.12.2000 to the 1.1.2001 over the stage go. As it halt no year 0 given has, comes the counting of 2000 years first only on the 31.12.2000 to an end. I make you this with a light to understand example out the allday clear: When you 2 kg sausage have will, can you from the butcher with fugue and right full 2000 grammes await and not only 1999. In this toghetherhang am I heavy beimpressed

ALLES GUTE FÜR Y2K!

from the people of Staffelstein, who with their mil-
lennium-celebrations one year wait will.

Great sorrows makes us the sonamed Y2K-problem,
as the computer-freaks short and boundy say. How
will our computers the time-jump from 1999 to 2000
behandle? Some of the older electronic comrades will
namley from 99 to 00 switch. And what this means,
can great problems after itself pull. Hundred-year-
olds are suddenly sucklings. And beaked beans in a
tin-box, holdbar until 2005, are now 95 years old.
Short and good, it will a world-wide bang-bang give.
All technology of the westly world will hopeless to-
gether-break. Good, when you then to byplay in
Africa are, milewide away from all civilization. If you
this chance not have, should you all important things
bunker – what to eat and to drink, money, benzine and
perhaps also a gas-cooker. I hear already the trappling
of the Apocalyptic Riders.

And when we overlive? What are the facts and
events of the old year, which we not simple to the acts
lay can, but which us in the next yearthousand really
of great help be will? First is it the Kilimandscharo,
which say and write four metres lower is than we always thought had. He is therewith only 5892 metres
high. Had you this for possible held? Second has us to
deepest overrushed, that a production-firm the film-
rights of Oskar Lafontaine's book "The heart beats
left" bougth has. We will see, if it Oscar-ripe is. When
man out such a dust-dry bacon a film make can, then
is it highest time, that the telephone-book of Munich
filmed is. Then have I tomindest a chance, endly as a
star in a film with to work.

ES WEIHNACHTET SEHR

Third must we our idea of colours correct: Electric stream is yellow, and the colour of money is black, teaches us our bimbes-chancellor, the Kohl Helmut. Fourth goes it about the Queen, who year for year her servants and lackeys out tradition a christmas-pudding tothinks. But his time has she this present not as always by Harrods bought, but in the cheaper supermarket Tesco. Clear, the Queen is poor like a churchmouse, and also the royal household has holes on all ends. For the future is it freely important, that the Queen much more money spare can, when she herself a customer-card by Tesco fetches and therethrough also the chance has, a trip to Brussels to win or a cost-free behandling on a beauty-farm.

So wide, so good. What I to Silvester make? As said, the year 2000 exists in reality not. I remain thathalf to home, with lots of bunkered things. As babysitter (as we in German say) make I the best thereout and good money. Five babies will I with safety in my if-hat take. Perhaps can I still two in the kitchen underbring.

I wish you all good for Y2K!

Your true Gisela

Politisches, allzu Politisches

The European House

AN MICHAIL GORBATSCHOW

Dear General Secretary!
Know you, that you a stone in the board by us Germans have? We love you formly and like to call you *Gorbi*. I hope, that you this cosy name right is. And all your books are bestsellers here. We read you more than Sandra Paletti, Uta Danella or Johannes Mario Simmel. When your folk you one day's not more as general secretary have will, can you safely from your books live.

The expressions *glasnost* and *perestroika,* which you hefound have, can we not more miss. We know not, what words we in earlier times therefor had. *Glasnost* and *perestroika* have thank your help in all our mouth-arts ingang found – be it in flat or high German, in Bavarian, Swabian or Saxon dialect. I know not, if you this beknown is. If not, then know you it now from competent side.

Special are we so happy over your idea of the European House. That means naturely, when you please a look in the atlas throw, that we Germans us direct in the middle of this house befind – and godbethank not in a dark, wet cellar or in a behelpmassy little room under the roof, where it in winter icy cold and in summer horribly hot is. Or have you as architect a good warmth-damming foreseen, perhaps also a penthouse with roof-garden and a noble outsight to all sides? Then is perhaps the middler etage not the best – let

– 207 –

POLITISCHES, ALLZU POLITISCHES

me afterthink. But the heating-costs are on every fall lower, when they under you and over you an orderly fire make. Is the cellar eventually a good bepieced wine-cellar?

Overhead would I like to see the ground-scratch of this house, better a little model. Is it a great villa, a gigantic block or more a rent-barrack? Questions over questions. Gives it also WGs in the house, where everyman make can, what he will, but nobody for the cleanness tostandy is? What for a house-order is accepted (Nato and/or Warsaw Pact), who shall pleasenice the housemaster play? Or will you all alone in the hand take? And what think you about one united Germany in the European House? Our Federal Chancellor, who absolute in the history-book will and on lovest also an architect were, has yes middler-while so an art clouds-cuckoo's home sketched, which perhaps not quite after your taste is ...

Quite important: Would you like your house? I ask you this, while namely the most architects not in the houses live, which they for others crimed have. I would me joy, what from you to hear.

Higheightingsfull

Your true Gisela Daum

P.S. I am sorry, that I you in English write. But this is a world-language, German yes not, and the world-language Russian can I overhead not!

– 208 –

Ballast of the Republic

ERICHS LAMPENLADEN

Dear Peter,

newly was I in Berlin. What has us there the old DDR only inbrocked! Now must we with immense parts of our income therefor upcome, that Berlin his outcome has. The Federal Finance Minister grips us deep in the pockets, and he shames himself not a bit. Othersides is our nice money with full hands out the window-thrown. Man knows yes middlerwhile, how so what goes. Like smeared.

Can we it in this situation tolet, that in Berlin unbethinged all from finest be shall? Yes, who are we then? Perhaps gold-donkeys? Thereby exist in the head-town so many old and usebar buildings, which not all down-pulled and on devil come out through complete new houses out-changed be must. Or?

One good example is the Palace of the Republic, under Berliners well beknown as Erich's Lamp-Shop, while namely alone in the ingang's hall over one thousand lamps hang. But the building looks not uglier out than other beton-castles from the seventies in east or west. Like the International Congress Centre (ICC), which to the self time built was, is it full-pumped with asbestos. Highest interesting in this togetherhang: For the sanitation of the ICC is enough money forehand, for the Palace ongively not. The one is a prestige-object, the other only a shabby memory out DDR times – a hated political symbol, which from the pic-

POLITISCHES, ALLZU POLITISCHES

ture-surface disappear must. Lover today than tomorrow. This argumentation oversees freely, that the power-havers in the DDR the same grounds into the field guided, when they his time the old Berliner Castle out the way roomed – a hated symbol out Prussia.

But nobody today has real the courage, the Palace of the Republic down to pull. The folk could halt quite nice sour be. With right. Special the East-Berliners love their *Palazzo Prozzi*, ifwell it now an architectonical zombie is. In this temple came earlier Hinz and Kunz together – fullcome freewilly, when you this what says. Here was always the bear loose – theatre, parties, shows and socialistic tralala. In this glass-box could you the balled glamour and glitter of the worker-and-farmer-state bewonder. Loud the Guinness Book brought the cooks a warm meal-time for 6000 visitors in 20 minutes on the table. Enormous, not true?

What shall now with the Palace of the Republic be? A Palace Hotel? The domicil of the Gauck-Office perhaps? Why not a prison with modernest punish-fulltrain? Before us nothing better infalls, should we the buildwork tomindest another name give: "Ballast of the Republic".

Your true Gisela

One hand washes the other

ÜBERALL AMIGOS AUF DER WELT

Dear Peter,

a friend, a good friend, that is the nicest, what it gives on the world. So sings wordwordly the folk's mouth heretolands, and right has he, the folk's mouth. In good days is it no problem, thousand friends to have. But when the life so right sad is, when you total down are and when you real not more in and out know, then comes the probe on the example. When it be must, gives a good friend his last shirt for you off. Thereupon can you gift take.

In public life is freely all a bit others. Politickers have no friends, they have amigos. This comes you Spanish fore? Hear to: An amigo is always stone-rich. He must in no situation on his last shirt back-grip. This sort of people has for usual all, what you think can, but they have nothing with politic on the hat. They besit a heap money, but no political power. When you always coal make must, stands you the sense not after political firlefanz.

Now to the politickers. They are in the rule so poor like a church-mouse. No wonder – the most of our politickers come out little relations, have nothing orderly learned and are for nothing others to use than for the politic. All too clever are they mostly not. Many of them have enough therewith to do, that they during their endless sittings not from the stool fall. This sort of people has the political power, but most

– 211 –

POLITISCHES, ALLZU POLITISCHES

not enough financial middles in besit. And for the political power alone can you yourself absolute nothing buy. Without money or bimbes (as the Kohl Helmut always said) is nothing loose. A hard truth.

It is now clear like thick ink, that there a balance bitter needy is. This belongs sotosay to our political culture. What the one not has, has the other in overflow. Where a will is, is always a way. When the politicker not so right liquid is, when him to byplay some financial speculations or transactions into the trousers gone are, grips him the amigo with a bit little-money under the arms.

Has but now the amigo some earnest problems, to byplay with the tax or with the build-right or with other strange ideas of the law, then should you see, what for a thankbar man the politicker be can. Seldom falls he real up thereby. One good word here for the amigo, one good word there. And it exist thousand tricks and feints, with money to juggle, special, when it black is. The wonders in the bible are nothing thereagainst. One hand washes the other.

Our Bavarian Free State can to byplay suddenly seventy million mark into the chimney write, which in ground the amigo as tax pay should. But this amigo whistles us what. He thinks in dream not thereon, his tax to pay. He has with his costbar money what others fore, to byplay his bimbes to a tax-oasis like Liechtenstein or Luxemburg to bring.

This system claps perfect, my dear friend and copper-stitcher. A politicker without amigos is like a bee without honey. But newerthings have it some of our political tandlers too wide driven. They could the

– 212 –

ÜBERALL AMIGOS AUF DER WELT

throat not full enough become. They should themselves what shame. One affair hunts the other, so that
the great F.J.S. – the protecting patron over our blue-
white amigo-land – in his grave rotates.

Your true Gisela

Kaiser Franz for Federal President!

EHRE, WEM EHRE GEBÜHRT

Dear Peter,

newly had the Kaiser Franz (born as Beckenbauer) his fiftieth birthday. Give the Kaiser, what the Kaiser's is. So came they from alll corners and ends of the earth and shook his hand and let him high-live. Now, as the circus a bit foreby is, make I me so my own thoughts over one of the greatest personalities, which wide and broad in sight are.

The Kaiser Franz is phenomenal. All world swarms still from his elegance, with which he the ball over the field and around the enemy dribbled. But also in frack and cylinder makes he always a good figure – be it in Bayreuth or on any gala in Munich. As golfer and dressman is he first cream. And his English has so a warm-hearty Bavarian undertone. Charming.

And there see you not one fold in his face. It is phantastic, how young the Kaiser with his fifty is. Thereagainst look the twens today total old out: dead with thirty, be-earthened with seventy. The Kaiser has also more juice and craft than all these blood-empty figures together, which these days their performance on the political stage give. Summa summarum: From head to foot is the Kaiser Franz a man of world and of format. Such an excellent man can you like a needle in the hay seek.

This brings me naturely on the idea, if not more in him sticks than a noble, but somehow also limited

– 214 –

EHRE, WEM EHRE GEBÜHRT

Football President. And with this meaning stand I not alone there. When shortly in a Hamburger week-leaf stood, that the Franz in future the new Bavarian cultusminister be shall, must I me freely wonder, what for a shit these north-lights together-write can. The great Kaiser Franz: soon a lousy upper-supervisor, who in every school the fore-written number of crosses controls? I think, my hamster needs a wood-leg!

What says my Aunt Lissy in so a situation? When already, then already. Minister President shall he be! What others comes overhead not in question – highest still the next President of the Federal Republic. When namely the Federal Roman soon the handcloth throws, is this post free. Before then the hick-hack with the political parties again loose goes, shall we Bavarians nails with heads make and our Kaiser Franz on the shield lift!

Yes, why not? The time is ripe, I say you: over-ripe. How formulates it a great philosopher? First look we once, then will we already see. Kaiser Franz for Federal President!

Beautifull greetings

His true Gisela

To the Oral Office, Washington D.C.

AN DEN AMERIKANISCHEN PRÄSIDENTEN

Dear Clinton Bill,
there sit you now quite nice in the ink – not so very as
political guide, but as the world's best-known apron-
hunter. In your place would I me freely nothing thereout make. Such peanuts can an American president
not from the stool throw. Where are we then? When
man bethinks, what for a hard job you for folk and fatherland do, must we all a bit after-sighted be. Every
man, special of your calibre and format, needs a little
short-while and some amusement from time to time.
And this fore all, when the Hillary tired is or when she
not each of your funny ideas good finds or with-make
will. There have you my fullest understanding. And
this must said be: You are not a heavy criminal and
also not the sin-buck of the whole nation.

Some people squeeze it but so out: The world is full
of problems, gives it not questions, which more important are? Hereto hear you from me a clear "no" .
Already our children will know: Where begins sex,
where hears it up, is oral sex "real" sex or is it more or
less like a lollipop? We have you to thank, that this
problem of greatest significance now endly worldwide
discussed is and not so very, what in this moment in
Russia, Albania, in the Iraq or with the Dow Jones
loose ist. Overthis am I yes so proud on you, that you
to every time known have, where the frontier was.
What always between you and the Lewinsky Monica

– 216 –

AN DEN AMERIKANISCHEN PRÄSIDENTEN

happened – no traffic. Hat off, that call I tactfull and fine-feeling.

Overhead the Monica – what for a fantastic girl! The Monica has us women, who a bit roundly are and too many kilos on the ribs have, shown, that we the hope not upgive should. Under the Kennedy John had we through-cutly types no chance had. Which woman is already a Marilyn Monroe? But the Monica has us in these days clear made, that also we poor sausages a proper man off-become and even a president on the angle-hook have can.

Is it now rigthy, that you "Billy the Liar" called are? Was it a heavy lie, when you said, there was nothing between you and the Monica? Even my old Aunt Lissy, who always very strict measure-sticks has, is of the meaning: It was only a little need-lie. When all men, who ever strange-went and thathalf lied have, before a TV-camera say must, that it them sorry does, then could 100 TV-senders in the next 100 years no other programme more bring. Will we that? And have you not already thousand times before God and the world said, that it you really very, very sorry does? But in my eyes have you the Castro Fidel forgotten. Please beg him: He should it you not evel-take, that the one or other Havanna with in the play was.

From our politickers here in Germany could you learn, how man such affairs elegant in the grip becomes. You must halt know: Our political headlings are for-true no innocence-lambs. I take as byplay only the Waigel Theo or the Schröder Gerhard. For a while were they naturely in all beat-lines with their wife-stories, but over short or long married they their side-

– 217 –

POLITISCHES, ALLZU POLITISCHES

jumps, so that the world again in order was. In the land of unlimited possibilities should this first right no problem be. Also for your money-sorrows is a brilliant solution in outsight. The Monica has yes already in outsight put, that she a wonderfull book over the whole story write will. That is it, all world needs much more details. When she the book-rights has and you the film-rights, then have you the little sheeps in the dry. I hope yes heavy, that you a lot of lusty videos in the Oral Office made have, which we one day's as a big film in our cinemas bewonder can. Know you still the tone-bands of the Nixon Richard — one of your fore-gangsters? The original material is simply the best.

You see, dear Bill, all is only half so terrible, as it out-looks: Head high, eyes wide shut and through!

Your true Gisela

Solo for King Edi

BAYERISCHER ASCHERMITTWOCH

Dear Peter,

how can I you explain, what *Fasching* is and what here
in these days loose was? To first must you this know:
In Germany gives it not only spring, summer, harvest
and winter, but also a fifth year-time between winter
and spring – the Carnival or *Fasching*, how we here in
the south of our fatherland say. To this time stands the
world head, the fools have the saying. Beggars can become kings and others round also. You must it you fol-
lowing-measures outpaint: A poor street-girl in London is suddenly Elizabeth II, and the Queen begives
herself as street-girl under the folk. Crazy, what? This
is freely only one single example. The people dress
themselves highest fantasy-rich or they have bynear
nothing on. They sing, drink and dance in excesses, let
the sow out and let the dear god a good man be. There
rules the purest chaos, what animalish fun makes.

But this lusty event goes not on until all eternity.
Unoutsoftly comes the great tomcat, and the name for
it is Ash Wednesday. This day marks normally the end
of the *Fasching*. The fools should after all the wild
time again to besensing come and from now on in sack
and ash go. As clear sightbar sign can you in the
church an ash-cross on the frontside of your head
off-fetch. But here in our blue-white republic go the
clocks complete different. Ash Wednesday is not
the day of sack and ash, but the high-point of the

– 219 –

POLITISCHES, ALLZU POLITISCHES

Fasching. It is the day of an undescribable murder's gaudi, and the beer flows in streams. Year for year comes it to the same political show-fight on Ash Wednesday. In Vilshofen meet the fans of the social democrats together and in Passau the onhangers of the christly socials. But in this year was all a bit others.

The Schröder Gerhard knew only too good, what from him in Bavaria expected is, when he himself to Vilshofen on the way made. For the first time came a Federal Chancellor to beseek. To the protesting farmers outside said he, that he in the pair weeks of his government not all repair can, what the christly democrats and socials in seventeen years total sowbagged have. On a rough block belongs a rough wedge. The greens let he know, that he not longer tosee will, that the tail with the dog waggles. For us Bavarians had he a special *schmankerl* with-brought: He promised a federal law for the beergarden-culture, if they in Munich this problem not loosen can. But when it so right against the Stoiber Edmund went, drove a flash down and laid the electricity of the hall lame. When this not a sign from heaven was ...

The better showmaster was naturely the Stoiber Edmund in the Nibelungen Hall in Passau, the greatest stem-table of the republic. Solo for King Edi. To the first time since the death of FJS spoke he namely alone on wide floor. To bring it short on the point: The shoes which the Edi there overtaken has, were a little bit too great. But I am safe, that he over short or long into these shoes grow will, when he in this style so wider makes.

– 220 –

BAYERISCHER ASCHERMITTWOCH

Three hours pulled the Edi against the sozis and the greens from the leather, what the clothes holds: "Schröder must way, way, way." So right sour was he also on his friend the Becker Boris, who together with the Haribo Thomas and the Müller-Westernhagen Marius in a campaign a word for the outlanders and the double-pass inlaid had. This called the Edi the "etage of champagne and caviar", whereagainst he himself for the "etage of liver-cheese" strong made. Was the Schröder for the beergarden-culture, so under-supported the Stoiber herewith the christly-eveninglandish culture, which he in danger sees, when it in a mishmash upgoes. The folk is in rage, and out the mass are posters high-held, on which to read is: "Edmund our Chancellor for 2002." The besaid stands on the table and grins like a honeycake-horse.

The end from the song? After such strong tobacco from all sides have I a tomcat, which himself washed has.

Your true Gisela

– 221 –

Not with us, with us not

STILLGESTANDEN, RICHTET EUCH!

Dear Peter,
you know safely, that Finland shortly the presidency
of the European Council from us Germans overtaken
has. And what happened in this moment? Our beautifull German speech – the speech of Immanuel Kant
and Johann Wolfgang von Goethe, the speech of
Heinrich Lummer, Alfred Dregger and Edmund
Stoiber – shall not more one of the official speeches
in the European conferences be.

Goes this with right things to? I believe, my hamster
yodels. Is this the thank for our permanent roll as
netto-payers in the European Union? Man does and
makes, man will yes not for eternal times the bad German be. There grip we the weak-bemiddled under the
arm, therewith they on a green branch come, and then
so what. Have the other Europeans overhead an idea
therefrom, how Europe without us outsee would? I
say you: A nice girland of countries with one big hole
in the middle.

You must you this in reality foreput: The official
conference-speeches are now English, French – and
Finnish! Why not equal Laplandish, Icelandish,
Greenlandish or Eskimo? I have nothing against the
Finlanders, but can you yourself a rhyme on this
make: *Semmoinen un Jörö-Jukka, Koikkakissy pörhö-
tukka. Tahto kynsiänsä säästää, muttei kampaa
päähän päästää?* It is finish, before you one single

– 222 –

STILLGESTANDEN, RICHTET EUCH!

word understand. The Finnish folk must an insee have, that it so not goes. Even Mika Häkkinen drives a German car.

Our German is a speech of clear words – special when it out the mouth of the Schröder Gerhard comes. The Chancellor said a clear "no" to such crooked tours. He will in future no German representatives more to the European conferences send. This shall the other Europeans themselves behind the ears write: With us can they not cat and mouse play, how it them into the head comes.The German conference-stool will so long empty be, until the Europeans again to reason come and the German speech endly the importance tocome let, which it in reality has. The greatest speech-community in Europe can not off-served be like a silly boy. There are we us united with the Austrians and number-rich Swiss landspeople. As compensation for this eclat could we highest accept, that the Scharping Rudolf the post of the general secretary of the NATO becomes. Then would all soldiers on his German commando hear: *Stillgestanden, richtet euch, die Augen geradeaus, links rum!*

As German time-companion can you the feeling have, not more gentleman in the own house to be. The Finnish is only the begin. When will the Netherlanders, the Danes and the Polish on the idea come, that our traffic-shields on the *Autobahn* tomindest in four speeches appear must? One good day's is the *Tagesschau* only still with Turkish subtitles to see. Yes, where live we then. To a certain degree are we horrible good-willy, but in such a form let we us not on

– 223 –

POLITISCHES, ALLZU POLITISCHES

the head about dance. It reaches fullcome, that so many English words in our speech inbroken are like a swarm of hay-horrors. What told me newly my friend Gerda? *Nachdem ich mein Ticket beim Einchecken vorgezeigt, das Shopping im Duty-Free hinter mir hatte und ganz easy zum Gate gegangen war, realisierte ich, daß mein Last-Minute-Flug von dieser funny Airline gecancelt war.*

Togiven, a little bit have we self guilt in this affair. Until the year of the lord 1972 were French and German the official conference-speeches in Brussels. Then came you British people into the European Union, and we Germans thought by us: How wonderfull, we all speak yes English! Inspired by William Tell said we: We will be one united folk of Anglophones. But the French saw this total others, their speech was together with English as conference-speech bybeholded. We Germans stepped byside and gave with our strange-speech-knowledges on. That have we now therefrom. What says my greatmother always? When man some body the little finger reaches, will he equal the whole hand have, if not the whole arm.

Your true Gisela

What will we more?

NACH EINEM JAHR DIE NASE VOLL

Dear Peter,

it lies now bynear one year back, that we the Kohl Helmut into the desert sent have. The Oggersheimer does me still a little bit sorry, but democracy is democracy and can towhilen very bitter be. The situation was the: The German folk had the nose stroken full. Sixteen years was the Christly Union on the rudder. Today can you of a sensation speak, when it a man and a wife so long together outhold. We thought, that it highest railway for a political change was. What too much is, is too much.

So lifted we the social democrats with their topman, the Schröder Gerhard, on the thrown. Well or evil must they the Greens with in the boat take. Now was the folk very spanned, how the new government the old problems in the grip become would. Very little-loud had they yes tolast inroomed, that they not every thing others, but many things better make would. New brooms sweep good – thought we.

Already after short time gave it a great awakening out all our dreams. These bloody beginners left no fat-pot out. Probing goes over studying. Today this, tomorrow that. Into the potatoes, out of the potatoes. In German say we: *Trial and error*. The chaos was perfect. This shall a tax-reform be? With all these hand-workly mistakes? Makes nothing, we start once more from front. The word "after-better" is the word oft he

POLITISCHES, ALLZU POLITISCHES

hour, perhaps the *Word of the Year*. A good byplay is also the planned end of the 630-DM-jobs. There gave it a great tumult in the whole land. But the new government said: Slowly, slowly, so have that not meant. How then?

In ground gives the new government the folk that, what the folk always wanted has – the feeling namely: Endly does itself what! But in reality? These newcomers have quite new methods developed. Was the Kohl Helmut beknown for his outsitting of problems, so let they now the problems themselves dead-run. There is dynamic in the play, there is what loose. They have a method found, the absolute stillstand as hectic activity to sell. So have we the inprint, that under Red-Green always the bear loose is. Under the Federal Helmut could you one year in bed remain, without that you what missed had. But now must you every minute hellish on the quivive be. Horrible, how it in the debate about the atom-exit thereunder and thereover went. And what came us one good day's to ears? Forget it all. In the afternoon was Schröder's interview from the morning already the snow from yesterday. From this hickhack has the folk now the nose full.

After my meaning is there groundsetly something not in order. Look, to become a florist, must you heretolands three years learn. Full three years must you through-exercise, some little moss-roses together to knot, so that it after what respectable outlooks. A sour bread. Learn-years are no master-years. Or the butchers – three years must they buffalo, what a cutlet is, what a schnitzel and what a bulette. Only the job of a

– 226 –

Federal Chancellor is after like before an unlearned job.

And where are the new ideas, where are the visions? Your Tony Blair has to byplay the vision, that the rich people not rich enough are. This can our social democrats naturely not on their flags write, ifwell they newerthings the little people quite nice bleed let. Some people say, the Schröder Gerhard has overhead no vision. That is complete nonsense. The Schröder Gerhard has all his visions *reached*, he is chancellor! More has he from life not wanted. More ambitions besits he not, there can we long wait. Since he the boss is, is he happy like a snow-king and grins like a honeycake-horse. The best picture gives the fun-chancellor always in TV off, but only when *he* the saying has: Look, I am here. When the RTL freely on the idea comes, him and his wife in the sending "How was I, Doris?" a little through the cacao to pull, then understands our highest fun-maker absolute no fun more. His majesty is not amused.

But all in all after one year: What will we more? More have we not earned.

Your true Gisela

From Christiane to Christina

WILLKOMMEN IN BERLIN!

Dear Peter,
I know not, if you already know: Our Federal President, the Duke Roman, has after five years his hat on the nail hanged. Thereby could he wider five years in his job tobring, if he only would and if the Federal Assembly nothing thereagainst had. But he has opensightly no lust more. Now can he himself his greatest wish of his life fullfill, namely with the Kohl Helmut near the Wolfgang-Lake after heart's lust frisbee play.

The new President is the Rough Johnny. His friends call him Brother John, while he so brotherly an open ear for every body has. This besaid Johnny Rough had also one greatest wish in his life, which with his election endly in fullfilling gone is. It was also highest railway. Some time-companions think yes, that he already too old is. I find this not, he is innerly still quite young. I think, that the most people him in their heart close will. Only our Christian Socials spat gift and gall after his election. They were stink-sour, while no body out their own rows a chance had. They should them what shame.

What is the job of a president? As we no monarchy in Germany have, is he so what like a Burger-King, who in first line the flag high to hold has. Black, red, gold. In the great politic may he not with-mix. But he can all nose long great speeches over god and the world swing. The Duke Roman was to byplay of the meaning, that through our folk a *ruck* go should. But the folk understood only railway-station and whistled him what. This should his after-follower a teaching be, before he what of fundamental importance to his folk says.

More than the Duke Roman will I freely his wife Christiane miss. The name of Rough Johnny's wife is at least Christina. But I pull very into doubt, if she the right person is, a federal-wide outbeamed cook-programme with similar sovereignty to guide. In her famous TV-show "To Guest by Christiane Duke" swung the First Lady the cook-spoon and drove her prominent guests over the mouth, that it a joy was. Standed man-pictures like the Hildebrandt Dieter or the Gottschalk Thomas were shorterhand to silly potato-peelers degraded. I have still picturely before eyes, how the charming Wickert Ulli three times started, a little anecdote to tell, and how he every time by the First Lady to silence brought was – between soup and tomato, without mercy. This has me very fallen.

Homely had I hoped, that now all important questions of the nation and of the world on the kitchen-table of Castle Bellevue come. I saw already the Clinton Bill in the Federal Kitchen, how he there the burnt pots and dirty pans to clean had – as punishment for all his sins and affairs. In my dreams saw I there also the star-kickers from the FC Bayern, condemned to cut mountains of onions – as punishment for their sow-stupidness in two cup-finals in one single year.

And now? Opensightly blows an other wind in Castle Bellevue. The Christina can with the three

POLITISCHES, ALLZU POLITISCHES

children in the gigantic building hide and seek play. Like Tarzan will the kids with their friends themselves from crown-lighter to crown-lighter swing. And outside can they on the flag-mast climb.

Heartly welcome in Berlin!

Your true Gisela

Germoney

NEUES AUS DER BIMBES-REPUBLIK

Dear Peter,
in Italy have they the mafia, in Germany have we the CDU. Know you, what this means? Cash Dealers United. So wide must it come. This christly honour-worth society had black contos in in- and outland and transported millions of bimbes in couverts and coffers through the world-history. From here to Switzerland, wider to Liechtenstein under the nice cover of "fence-king" and back to Germany. It functioned as good-organized money-washing, and the criminal energy was not from bad parents. But us all was the bear upbound, this money came from noble spenders out jewish circles!

Now will the poor Schäuble Wolfgang light into the dark bring. Thereby has he self dirt on the stick. Can a buck – now the gardener – this sow-stall outmist? First has he 100 000 DM from a dubious weapon-handler taken and then has he in the Federal Day about this not the truth said. Gives it more solid grounds for a backstep?

Then is it highest astonishing, how the members of this honour-worth club react, when it them on the collar goes. The strategy is: I know of nothing; my name is hare, I live in the clover. The Rühe Volker to byplay is so one. He says frank and free, he knows nothing over the black bimbes. He knows not even, that he in the questionly time general secretary of the CDU was.

– 231 –

POLITISCHES, ALLZU POLITISCHES

How can we in these days know, who the truth speaks
and who the blue only so from heaven lies? In end-ef-
fect comes the truth only *Schäuble* for *Schäuble* to the
day's light. Every day a new sensation. How many
slices can you from a salami cut?

One part of the besaid strategy is: First when it not
more others goes, when it all sparrows from the roofs
whistle, when it next day in every newspaper stands,
then can you so slowly togive, that you your fingers
dirty made have. But, please, speak never of a criminal
act. Never. Say only, that you a "mistake" made have –
so, as if you forgotten had, that *Schifffahrt* newerthings with three *f* to write is. And then must you
also say: I hold this "drive-hunt" not one day longer
out. This is o-tone from one of our highest clean-men,
the Kanther Manfred, who his time as inner minister
every black-driver in a bus on lovest on the spot behind
Swedish curtains brought had. In reality besits this
self-named black sheriff no feeling for law and order.
But these gangsters shame themselves not. They had
overhead no scruples – always Kiep smiling.

The upperest wire-puller is naturely the Kohl Helmut, his sign's bimbes-chancellor, who out our fatherland the Bimbes-Republic Germoney made has. This
thick-head will partout not the names of the spenders
price-give. He says us not even the name of his soap-
spender. It is possible, that it smear-soap is. What are
this for "respectable burgers", who him millions of
bimbes given have and now friend Helmut in the rain
stand let? Or has this all a criminal background?

The bimbes-chancellor says, that he horse and rider
not name can, while he the spenders his big "honour-

– 232 –

word" given has, the cat not out the sack to let. I think,
I hear not right: "Honour-word"! After the Barschel-
affair had I thought, that no body more this begrip so
quick in the mouth takes. It is the height: A criminal
"honour-word" stands now higher than right and law,
which into-hold our old-chancellor high-holy oaths
sworn has! With three fingers to heaven – so true him
God helps. You see: A whole party and the earlier chief
are from all good ghosts left.

And now? After the first shock goes a whole nation
to the day's order over. One milllion here, two millions
there, eight millions for the lady *Hü-Bü* out the De-
fence Ministry, eleven (in French: elf) millions for a
cow-handle in Leuna – what shall's? It makes nothing.
Little people hangs man, the great lets man run. Eyes
shut and through! The tooth of time, which so many
tears dried has, will also over this wound grass grow let.
Really?

Your true Gisela

Ausführliches Inhaltsverzeichnis

Zum Geleit 7

Vorwort des Herausgebers 9

Moderne Zeiten

What is lifestyle?	13	Fast eine Lebens-beratung
Beer on wine	16	Ein gutes Tröpfchen
A picture for the gods	19	Pizza: Tag und Nacht
The undergang of the evening-land	22	Die neue Kultur des Essens
The purest terror	25	Wenn das Telefon klingelt
You, I am now here	27	Segen und Fluch des Handy
Place there, now come I!	30	Geländewagen oder: *Off-Road*
Nothing like away from here	32	Auf zum Ballermann
You can say you to me	35	Englisch? Nichts leichter als das!
They whistle you what!	38	Neues Bauen in der Kritik

– 234 –

AUSFÜHRLICHES INHALTSVERZEICHNIS

Freud und Leid im Alltag

Out of the tailor	43	Sechs Richtige im Lotto
Big Brother lets greet	45	Reklame, Reklame, Reklame
The last bite the dogs	47	Hunde, wollt ihr ewig leben?
Total oldmodish	49	Loblied auf das Fahrrad
Ripe for the clap's mill?	51	Tomaten haben eine Seele
All for the cat	53	Erlebnis an der Tankstelle
When the cock crows on the mist	55	Weisheit des Wetterberichts
Am I now a CallGirl?	57	Die grauen Zellen der Telekom

Britischer geht's nicht

Find you that right?	63	An einen berühmten Detektiv
A horrible train through the window	65	Giselas England-Abenteuer
In null comma nothing	68	Invasion durch den Tunnel?
Pistol on the breast	70	An einen britischen Premier
Man makes what through	72	EG-Normen für England?

AUSFÜHRLICHES INHALTSVERZEICHNIS

From woman to woman	74	Gisela faßt sich ein Herz
Gun by foot	76	Die Sorge um den Thronfolger
I and the Queen	80	Als das Wünschen noch geholfen hat
Bethink it, oh soul!	82	An einen Buchclub in England
Total on the woodway	84	Deutsche Sprache, schwere Sprache?

Deutsches Wesen und die Welt

Order must be	89	„DIN" geht über alles
The yellow from the egg	91	Deutsche Gemütlich-keit
I am not an outlander	94	Die Deutschen als geborene Inländer
After us the sin-flood	97	Wo ist die Mauer?
A devil will I do!	99	Deutsche Rechtschreib-reform
You dear sky!	101	Der Gartenzwerg als Kulturgut
We are again who	104	Dank Daimler und dank Guildo
With four boys is it easy	106	Wie geht eigentlich Skat?
Self is the man	109	Ein Volk von Heim-werkern
The holy mass	111	Unsere Dichter und Denker

AUSFÜHRLICHES INHALTSVERZEICHNIS

Gesund und schön

The inner swine-dog	117	Zwischen Fitness und Wellness
Train for train	120	Raucher aller Länder, vereinigt euch!
Nothing goes over jogging!	122	Grundzüge einer Weltanschauung
Venus from Kilo	124	Zuviel Speck auf den Knochen
The po in bestform	126	Allerwerteste Probleme
Fat swims above	128	Nie wieder oder immer wieder?
This wool on the head!	130	Täglicher Kampf mit borstigen Zotteln
The wandering is the miller's lust	132	Mit Gesang durch die Natur
Helps a cure-shadow?	135	Morgens Fango, abends Tango

Ökologie für den Hausgebrauch

Let mother nature grow!	139	Kraut und Rüben
Full in the trousers	141	Der Fluch der guten Tat
Bird of the Year	143	Tante Lissy hat Geburtstag
Green is the hope	145	Ein X für ein U
It greens so green	147	Architektentrost

AUSFÜHRLICHES INHALTSVERZEICHNIS

Green Point and Yellow Sack	150	Die Freuden der Müll-trennung
It stinks to heaven	152	Vom Regen in die Traufe
Eat-culture?	154	Schwerverdauliches

Liebe, Lust und Frust

The cat in the sack?	159	Gisela antwortet auf eine Heiratsanzeige
I silly cow	162	Diese oder jene Beziehungskiste
When is a man a man?	165	Die neue Männer-bewegung
I mean it only good	168	Scheidung vorprogram-miert?
Can that good-go?	171	Steffi und die Liebe

Direkt aus der Traumfabrik

So what comes from so what	177	„Eine verhängnisvolle Affäre"
... that the walls only so wobble	179	Erst kriegen, dann bekriegen sie sich
And when they not dead are ...	181	Einfach herzzerreißend

– 238 –

AUSFÜHRLICHES INHALTSVERZEICHNIS

Weeping like a castle-dog	183	Die Urgewalt der „Titanic"
Holy straw-sack!	185	Wie es der Zufall so will

Es weihnachtet sehr

Christmas-tree on the back-train?	191	Die Lehren der Weihnachtsökologie
Sweeter the bells never cling	193	Voll im Weihnachtsstreß
From heaven high	195	Diverse Wünsche zum Fest
Joseph & Jesus	197	Neue berufliche Alternativen
All years again	199	Weihnachten im Internet
Bang-bang	202	Alles Gute für Y2K!

Politisches, allzu Politisches

The European House	207	An Michail Gorbatschow
Ballast of the Republic	209	Erichs Lampenladen
One hand washes the other	211	Überall Amigos auf der Welt
Kaiser Franz for Federal President!	214	Ehre, wem Ehre gebührt

– 239 –

AUSFÜHRLICHES INHALTSVERZEICHNIS

To the Oral Office, Washington D.C.	216	An den amerikanischen Präsidenten
Solo for King Edi	219	Bayerischer Aschermittwoch
Not with us, with us not	222	Stillgestanden, richtet euch!
What will we more?	225	Nach einem Jahr die Nase voll
From Christiane to Christina	228	Willkommen in Berlin!
Germoney	231	Neues aus der Bimbes-Republik